National Contract Management Association
21740 Beaumeade Circle, Suite 125
Ashburn, Virginia 20147
www.ncmahq.org
(800) 344-8096

ISBN 978-0-940343-90-0

Contents

Certified Federal Contracts Manager

Study Gu...

SECOND E...

About the National Contract Management Association

The National Contract Management Association (NCMA) was formed in 1959 to foster the professional growth and educational advancement of its members. NCMA is a membership-based professional society whose leadership is composed of volunteer officers.

NCMA is devoted to education and training, to research and study, and to a certification program that reflects the highest standards of professional achievement. Guided by a code of ethics, the association is committed to developing and providing programs, products, and services that nurture and enhance contract management competencies through leadership and business management partnering.

Thousands of professionals enhance their knowledge and leverage opportunities in purchasing, procurement, project management, and contract management with NCMA. Comprised of individual members and professional groups from nonprofit, industry, and government, NCMA provides unique resources for the contracting community.

For more than 50 years, members have taken advantage of NCMA membership benefits to advance their careers. Practical, proven survival techniques and industry news help members stay informed about current contract management events. NCMA continues to provide vital information about the career field through the association's prestigious publications, educational materials, and professional resources.

NCMA is located at 21740 Beaumeade Circle, Suite 125, Ashburn, Virginia 20147. The NCMA office is open Monday through Friday between the hours of 8:30am and 5:00pm ET. Please visit our website at **www.ncmahq.org**

The NCMA Vision, Mission, and Values

I. Our Vision

NCMA will lead and represent the contract management profession. Our vision is that enterprises will succeed through improved buyer–seller relationships based on common values, practices, and professional standards.

II. Our Mission

NCMA's mission is to improve organizational performance through effective contract management.

III. Our Value Propositions

- NCMA provides the tools, resources, and leadership opportunities to enhance each member of the profession's performance, career, and accomplishments.

- NCMA provides the structure, name recognition, and products directly and through local chapters to contracting professionals worldwide.

- NCMA provides employers ready access to skilled human capital, learning resources, best practices, standards, and metrics of the profession.

- We enable other entities—such as researchers, consultants, trainers, recruiters, advertisers, and universities—to gain broad access to defined segments of our community of practice and our Body of Knowledge for the purpose of advancing the profession and fulfilling their individual goals.

IV. Our Values

We are committed to

- Principled professional conduct and achievement, as dictated by the Contract Management Code of Ethics;

- An open exchange of ideas in a neutral forum;

- A culturally and professionally diverse membership;

- Excellence in everything we do, especially our service to our members and the contract management community;

- Continuing education, training, and leadership opportunities through a network of local chapters;

- Remaining the preeminent source of professional development for contract professionals;

- Recognizing and rewarding professional excellence and superior individual achievement in support of the contract management profession;

- Demonstrated professional achievement through certification;

- Quality volunteer leadership; and

- Members' highly principled freedom of action and responsibility to the people and organizations they serve.

Contract Management Code of Ethics

Each member of the contract management profession accepts the obligation to continuously improve one's professional knowledge and job performance in the field of contract management, and to abide by the letter and spirit of the ethical standards set forth below.

Each member of NCMA shall:

1. Strive to attain the highest professional standard of job performance, to exercise diligence in carrying out one's professional duties, and to serve the profession to the best of one's ability.

2. Conduct oneself in such a manner as to bring credit upon the profession, as well as to maintain trust and confidence in the integrity of the contract management process.

3. Avoid engagement in any transaction that might conflict or appear to conflict with the proper discharge of one's professional duties by reason of a financial interest, family relationship, or any other circumstances.

4. Comply with all laws and regulations that govern the contract management process in the jurisdictions in which one conducts business, including protection of competition-sensitive and proprietary information from inappropriate disclosure.

5. Keep informed of developments in the contract management field, utilizing both formal training and ad hoc means, to continuously increase knowledge, skill, and professional competence.

6. Share one's knowledge and experience openly to contribute to the development of other professionals, improve performance quality, and enhance public perception of the profession.

7. Not knowingly influence others to commit any act that would constitute a violation of this code.

Acknowledgements

NCMA gives special recognition to **Judith A. Ballou, Fellow,** for her exceptional effort in subject matter review and editing of the *CFCM Study Guide, 2nd Edition*.

NCMA also acknowledges the contributions of the following members of the *CFCM Study Guide* Project:

Adam Goldstein, CPCM, CFCM, Fellow

Clint Paulson, J.D., CPCM, CFCM, CCCM

Christopher Robey, CPCM, CFCM, CCCM, Fellow

Eugene Scott, J.D., CPCM, CFCM, CCCM

Evan Thorpe, CFCM

Courtney Kappel Tilque, CFCM

Michelle Warren, CFCM

Etta Waugh, CPCM, CFCM

Introduction

The CFCM certification is awarded to candidates who meet rigorous standards, including experience, education, training, and knowledge. It is a professional designation of distinction and carries the respect of one's peers in the profession. NCMA certifications are competency-based, legally defensible, and are based on psychometrically sound objective examination of knowledge. The NCMA professional certification program is designed to elevate professional standards, enhance individual performance, and distinguish those who demonstrate knowledge essential to the practice of contract management.

The best way to study for an examination is to participate in a structured study group. NCMA offers a 10-week, instructor-led online course to assist candidates in preparing for the exam. Candidates who cannot take the 10-week course may find it helpful to join or start a local study group. In the absence of such a group, this study guide, along with *The Desktop Guide to Basic Contracting Terms* and the *Federal Acquisition Regulation (FAR)*, should provide sufficient material for an experienced contracts professional to achieve success on the CFCM examination through self-study.

This study guide has been updated to incorporate changes up to and including Federal Acquisition Circular FAC 2005-57 effective March 15, 2012 and FAC 2005-56 effective April 2, 2012. It provides the candidate with a detailed study outline of the main topics within each *FAR* part and includes specific references. Once you feel adequately prepared for the examination, you can test your knowledge by taking the practice test included herein and grading it with the answer key provided.

The practice test is designed to both facilitate review and allow the opportunity to assess personal mastery of topics addressed in the CFCM examination. Although questions on the practice test may be similar to those on the examination, study of the detailed outline or memorization of the questions on the practice test is not sufficient preparation for the examination.

NOTE: The CFCM Examination is subject to continual updates to reflect additions, deletions, and changes in the *Federal Acquisition Regulation*. The *CFCM Study Guide* is updated on roughly an 18-month cycle. CFCM candidates are responsible for any new material printed in the Federal Acquisition Circulars and incorporated into the *FAR* subsequent to the publication of this study guide.

If you have any comments on the structure or material contained within this study guide, please e-mail them to **certification@ncmahq.org**.

Section

ONE

FAR Parts 1–9, 16–18

A. Purpose, Authority, Issuance (FAR 1.1)

The Federal Acquisition Regulations System was established for the codification and publication of uniform policies and procedures for acquisition by all executive agencies. The Federal Acquisition Regulations System consists of the *Federal Acquisition Regulation (FAR)*, which is the primary document, and agency acquisition regulations that implement or supplement the *FAR*.

Statement of Guiding Principles (FAR 1.102)

The vision for the Federal Acquisition System is to deliver on a timely basis the best value product or service to the customer, while maintaining the public's trust and fulfilling public policy objectives. Participants in the acquisition process should work together as a team and should be empowered to make decisions within their area of responsibility.

Performance Standards (FAR 1.102-2)
The Federal Acquisition System will

1. Satisfy the customer in terms of cost, quality, and timeliness of the delivered product or service;

2. Minimize administrative operating costs;

3. Conduct business with integrity, fairness, and openness; and

4. Fulfill public policy objectives.

Acquisition Team (FAR 1.102-3)
The Acquisition Team consists of all participants in government acquisition, including not only representatives of the technical, supply, and procurement commu-

1

nities, but also the customers they serve and the contractors who provide the products and services.

Role of the Acquisition Team (FAR 1.102-4)

The members of the team are empowered to make decisions and act within their areas of responsibility consistent with the Guiding Principles. Authority and accountability will be delegated to the lowest level allowed by law. The government is committed to providing training and resources to maintain and improve the knowledge, skills, and ability of its team members and encourages contractors to provide the same resources to its members. This system will encourage a cooperative relationship between the government and contractors consistent with its responsibility to the taxpayers. If a policy, procedure, strategy, or practice is in the best interest of the government and is not specifically addressed in the *FAR* or prohibited by law, executive order, or regulation, government members of the team should not assume it is prohibited. Absence of direction should be interpreted as permitting the team to innovate and use sound business judgment that is consistent with law and within the limits of their authority. Contracting officers should take the lead in encouraging business process innovation and ensuring that sound business decisions are made.

Authority, Applicability, Issuance, OMB Approval, and Certifications (FAR 1.103-7)

The Office of Federal Procurement Policy Act of 1974 as amended by Public Law 96-83 gives the *FAR* its authority. The *FAR* is prepared, issued, and maintained and the *FAR* System prescribed by the Secretary of Defense, the Administrator of General Services, and the Administrator of the National Aeronautics and Space Administration under their statutory authorities. The *FAR* governs all acquisitions described in FAR Part 2 unless expressly excluded.

The *FAR* is published in several manners and places and adheres to a specific numbering scheme in the arrangement of its regulations. Each clause is divided, as necessary, into a part, subpart, section, and subsection, and is further subdivided as needed with alphanumeric subdivisions. The specific details regarding the numbering system are described in FAR Part 1.105.

The Paperwork Reduction Act of 1980 requires federal agencies to obtain approval from the Office of Management and Budget (OMB) before collecting information from 10 or more members of the public. The OMB control numbers for each *FAR* segment are listed in FAR 1.106.

A contractor or offeror may not be required under this section to provide a new certification unless it is mandated by statute or the Administrator for Federal Procurement Policy approves the requirement.

FAR Conventions (FAR 1.108)

The following conventions provide guidance for interpreting the *FAR*:

Words and Terms: Definitions in Part 2 apply to the entire regulation unless specifically defined in another part, subpart, section, provision, or clause. Words or terms defined in a specific part, subpart, section, provision, or clause have that meaning when used in that part, subpart, section, provision, or clause. Undefined words retain their common dictionary meaning.

Delegation of Authority: Each authority is delegable unless specifically stated otherwise. (FAR 1.102-4(b))

Dollar Thresholds: Unless otherwise specified, a specific dollar threshold for the purpose of applicability is the final anticipated dollar value of the action, including the dollar value of all options. If the action establishes a maximum quantity of supplies or services to be acquired or establishes a ceiling price or establishes the final price to be based on future events, the final anticipated dollar value must be the highest final priced alternative to the government, including the dollar value of all options.

Application of *FAR* Changes to Solicitations and Contracts: Unless otherwise specified (a) *FAR* changes apply to solicitations issued on or after the effective date of the change; (b) contracting officers may, at their discretion, include the *FAR* changes in solicitations issued before the effective date, provided award of the resulting contract(s) occurs on or after the effective date; and (c) contracting officers may, at their discretion, include the changes in any existing contract with appropriate consideration.

Citations: When the *FAR* cites a statute, executive order, Office of Management and Budget circular, Office of Federal Procurement Policy letter, or relevant portion of the *Code of Federal Regulations*, the citation includes all applicable amendments, unless otherwise stated.

Imperative Sentences: When an imperative sentence (containing verbs such as shall, must, or will) directs action, the contracting officer is responsible for the action, unless another party is expressly cited.

Statutory Acquisition-related Dollar Thresholds—Adjustment for Inflation (FAR 1.109)

As required in the U.S. Code (U.S.C.), the *FAR* Council must adjust all statutory acquisition-related dollar thresholds in the *FAR* for inflation. This adjustment is calculated every five years, beginning in October 2005, using the Consumer Price Index. Acquisition-related dollar thresholds established by the Davis-Bacon Act, the Service Contract Act of 1965, or the U.S. Trade Representative pursu-

ant to the authority of the Trade Agreements Act of 1979 are not, however, subject to the USC statute regarding escalation.

B. Administration (FAR 1.2)

Revisions to the *FAR* are coordinated through two councils. The *Defense Acquisition Regulations* (*DAR*) Council shall include representatives of all military departments, the Defense Logistics Agency, and the National Aeronautics and Space Administration. The Civilian Agency Acquisition (CAA) Council shall include representatives from the Departments of Agriculture, Homeland Security, Interior, Labor, State, Transportation, and Treasury, as well as the Environmental Protection Agency, Social Security Administration, Small Business Administration, and the Department of Veterans Affairs. The chairperson for the *DAR* Council will be a representative for the Secretary of Defense and the chairperson for the CAA shall be the representative of the Administrator of General Services.

The General Services Administration shall establish a *FAR* Secretariat to print, publish, and distribute the *FAR* through the Code of Federal Regulations and shall provide centralized administrative services and support for both councils.

Agency compliance with the *FAR* is the responsibility of the Secretary of Defense for military departments and defense agencies and the responsibility of the Administrator of General Services for civilian agencies other than NASA, and the Administrator of NASA for NASA activities.

C. Agency Acquisition Regulations (FAR 1.3)

Agency acquisition regulations shall be limited to those necessary to implement *FAR* policy and procedures within the agency and additional policies, procedures, solicitation provisions, or contract clauses that supplement the *FAR* to satisfy the specific needs of the agency.

D. Deviations from the *FAR* (FAR 1.4)

Unless precluded by law, executive order, or regulation, deviations from the *FAR* may be granted to meet the specific needs and requirements of each agency.

1. Individual deviations (1.403). Individual deviations affect only one contract action, and unless 1.405(e) is applicable, may be authorized by the agency head. The contracting officer must document the justification and agency approval in the contract file.

2. Class deviations (1.404). Class deviations affect more than one contract action. When an agency knows that it will require a class deviation on a permanent basis, it should propose a *FAR* revision, if appropriate. Civilian agencies, other than NASA, must furnish a copy of each approved class deviation to the *FAR* Secretariat.

   a. For civilian agencies other than NASA, class deviations may be authorized by agency heads or their designees, unless 1.405(e) is applicable. Delegation of this authority shall not be made below the head of a contracting activity. Authorization of class deviations by agency officials is subject to the following limitations:

      1. An agency official who may authorize a class deviation, before doing so, shall consult with the chairperson of the Civilian Agency Acquisition Council (CAA Council), unless that agency official determines that urgency precludes such consultation.

      2. Recommended revisions to the *FAR* shall be transmitted to the *FAR* Secretariat by agency heads, or their designees, for authorizing class deviations.

   b. For DOD, class deviations shall be controlled, processed, and approved in accordance with the *Defense FAR Supplement.*

   c. For NASA, class deviations shall be controlled and approved by the Assistant Administrator for Procurement. Deviations shall be processed in accordance with agency regulations.

E. Agency and Public Participation (FAR 1.5)

Agency and public comments will be sought for significant changes to the *FAR*. Unsolicited proposals for changes may be submitted for consideration. Where it is deemed beneficial, public meetings may be held.

F. Career Development, Contracting Authority, and Responsibilities (FAR 1.6)

Unless specifically prohibited by another provision of law, authority and responsibility to contract for authorized supplies and services are vested in the agency head. The agency head may establish contracting activities and delegate broad authority to manage the agency's contracting functions to the heads of such contracting activities. Contracts may be entered into and signed on behalf of the government only by contracting officers. In some agencies, a relatively small number of high-level officials are designated contracting officers solely by virtue of their positions. Contracting officers below the level of a head of a contracting activity shall be selected and appointed.

Contracting officers have authority to enter into, administer, or terminate contracts, and make related determinations and findings; however, they may bind the government only to the extent of the authority delegated to them.

Contracting officers are not to enter into contracts unless all requirements of law, executive orders, regulations, and other applicable procedures, including clearances and approvals, have been met.

Unauthorized commitments are agreements that are not binding solely because the government representative who made it lacked the authority to enter into that agreement on behalf of the government. Agencies should take positive action to preclude, to the maximum extent possible, the need for ratification actions. Although procedures are provided in this section for use in those cases where the ratification of an unauthorized commitment is necessary, these procedures may not be used in a manner that encourages such commitments being made by government personnel.

Ratification is the act of approving an unauthorized commitment. Unauthorized commitments may be ratified when

- Supplies or services have been provided to and accepted by the government, or the government otherwise has obtained or will obtain a benefit resulting from performance of the unauthorized commitment;

- The resulting contract would otherwise have been proper if made by an appropriate contracting officer;

- The contracting officer determines the price to be fair and reasonable;

- The contracting officer recommends payment and legal counsel concurs in the recommendation;

- Funds are available and were available at the time the unauthorized commitment was made, and

- The ratification is in accordance with any other limitations prescribed under agency procedures.

Contracting officers are to be appointed in writing on an SF 1402, certificate of appointment, which must state any limitations on the scope of authority to be exercised, other than limitations contained in applicable law or regulation. While individuals delegated micropurchase authority need not be appointed on an SF 1402, they must be appointed in writing.

The contracting officer is required to designate and authorize, in writing, a contracting officer's representative (COR) to assist in the technical monitoring or administration of contracts and orders other than those that are firm-fixed price, and for firm-fixed-price contracts and orders, as appropriate. A COR must be a government employee, unless otherwise authorized in agency regulations; be qualified by training and experience commensurate with the responsibilities to be delegated; and be certified and maintain certification. The COR has no authority to make any commitments or changes that affect price, quality, quantity, delivery, or other terms and conditions of the contract.

G. Determinations and Findings (FAR 1.7)

1.701 Definition
Determinations and findings (D&F) means a special form of written approval by an authorized official that is required by statute or regulation as a prerequisite to taking certain contract actions. The "determination" is a conclusion or decision supported by the "findings." The findings are statements of fact or rationale essential to support the determination and must cover each requirement of the statute or regulation.

1.702 General and 1.703 Class Determinations and Findings
A D&F shall ordinarily be for an individual contract action, however, unless otherwise

prohibited, class D&Fs may be executed for classes of contract actions. A class may consist of contract actions for the same or related supplies or services or other contract actions that require essentially identical justification. (FAR 1.702(a) FAR 1.703(a))

FAR 1.704 Content

At a minimum, a D&F must contain identification of the agency and of the contracting activity and specific identification of the document as a D&F; nature and/or description of the action being approved; citation of the appropriate statute and/or regulation upon which the D&F is based; findings that detail the particular circumstances, facts, or reasoning essential to support the determination; a determination, based on the findings, that the proposed action is justified under the applicable statute or regulation; an expiration date of the D&F, if required; the signature of the official authorized to sign the D&F; and the date signed.

FAR 1.706 Expiration

Expiration dates are required for class D&Fs, but optional for individual D&Fs. (FAR 1.706)

FAR Part 2. Definitions of Words and Terms

A. Definitions (FAR 2.1)

Common words often have special, specific meaning in the *FAR*. The definitions below are often used throughout the *FAR*. This list of terms should not be considered the sole terminology that a contract manager needs, thus your study should include a careful reading of these and other definitions found in the *FAR*.

Acquisition: Acquiring by contract with appropriated funds, supplies, or services (including construction) by and for the use of the federal government through purchase or lease, whether they are already in existence or must be created, developed, demonstrated, and evaluated. Acquisition begins at the point when agency needs are established and includes all activities to include technical and management functions directly related to the process of fulfilling agency needs by contract.

Advisory and Assistance Services: Those services provided under contract by nongovernmental sources to support or improve organizational policy development, decision-making, management and administration, program and/or project management and administration, or R&D activities. All advisory and assistance services are classified in one of the following subdivisions: management and professional support services; studies, analyses, and evaluations; or engineering and technical services.

Best Value: The expected outcome of an acquisition that, in the government's estimation, provides the greatest overall benefit in response to the requirement.

Bundled Contract: A contract where the requirements have been consolidated by bundling.

Bundling:

    a. Consolidating two or more requirements for supplies or services, previously provided or performed under separate smaller contracts, into a solicitation for a single contract that is likely to be unsuitable for award to a small business concern due to

        1. The diversity, size, or specialized nature of the elements of the performance specified;

        2. The aggregate dollar value of the anticipated award;

        3. The geographical dispersion of the contract performance sites; or

        4. Any combination of these factors.

b. "Separate smaller contract" as used in this definition, means a contract that has been performed by one or more small business concerns or that was suitable for award to one or more small business concerns.

c. This definition does not apply to a contract that will be awarded and performed entirely outside of the United States.

Claim: A written demand or written assertion by one of the contracting parties seeking, as a matter of right, the payment of money in a sum certain, the adjustment or interpretation of contract terms, or other relief arising under or relating to the contract. However, a written demand or written assertion by the contractor seeking the payment of money exceeding $100,000 is not a claim under the Contract Disputes Act of 1978 until certified as required by the act. A voucher, invoice, or other routine request for payment that is not in dispute when submitted is not a claim. The submission may be converted to a claim, by written notice to the contracting officer as provided in 33.206(a), if it is disputed either as to liability or amount or is not acted upon in a reasonable time.

Commercial Item:

a. Any item, other than real property, that is of a type customarily used for nongovernmental purposes and that has been sold, leased, or licensed to the general public; or has been offered for sale, lease, or license to the general public;

b. Any item that evolved from an item described in paragraph (a) of this definition through advances in technology or performance and that is not yet available in the commercial marketplace, but will be available in the commercial marketplace in time to satisfy the delivery requirements;

c. Any item that would satisfy a criterion expressed in paragraphs (a) or (b) of this definition, but for

1. Modifications of a type customarily available in the commercial marketplace; or

2. Minor modifications of a type not customarily available in the commercial marketplace made to meet federal government requirements. "Minor" modifications do not significantly alter the nongovernmental function or essential physical characteristics of an item or component, or change the purpose of a process.

d. Any combination of items meeting the requirements of paragraphs (a), (b), (c), or (e) of this definition that are of a type customarily combined and sold in combination to the general public.

e. Installation services, maintenance services, repair services, and training services, if such services are procured for support of an item referred to in paragraphs (a), (b), (c), or (d) of this definition.

f. Services of a type offered and sold competitively in substantial quantities in the commercial marketplace based on established catalog or market prices for specific tasks performed or specific outcomes to be achieved under the standard commercial terms and conditions. This does not include services that are sold based on hourly rates without an established catalog or market price for a specific service performed or specific outcome to be achieved.

g. Any item, combination of items, or service referred to in paragraphs (a) through (f) herein, notwithstanding the fact that the item, combination of items, or service is transferred between or among separate divisions, subsidiaries, or affiliates of a contractor; or

h. A nondevelopmental item, if the procuring agency determines the item was developed exclusively at private expense and sold in substantial quantities, on a competitive basis, to multiple state and local governments.

Contract: A mutually binding legal relationship obligating the seller to furnish supplies or services (including construction) and the buyer to pay for them. It includes all types of commitments that obligate the government to an expenditure of appropriated funds and that, except as otherwise authorized, are in writing. In addition to bilateral instruments, contracts include but are not limited to awards and notices of awards; job orders or task letters issued under basic ordering agreements; letter contracts; orders such as purchase orders, under which the contract becomes effective by written acceptance or performance; and bilateral contract modifications. Contracts do not include grants and cooperative agreements.

Contracting: Purchasing, renting, leasing, or otherwise obtaining supplies or services from nonfederal sources. Contracting includes description (but not determination) of supplies and services required and solicitation of sources, preparation and award of contracts, and all phases of contract administration. It does not include making grants or cooperative agreements.

Contracting Officer (CO): A person with the authority to enter into, administer, and/or terminate contracts and make related determinations and findings. The term includes certain authorized representatives of the CO acting within the limits of their authority as delegated by the CO (i.e., administrative contracting officer (ACO) and termination contracting officer (TCO)).

Electronic Commerce: Electronic techniques for accomplishing business transactions including electronic mail or messaging, World Wide Web technology, electronic bulletin boards, purchase cards, electronic funds transfer, and electronic data interchange.

Indirect Cost Rate: The percentage or dollar factor that expresses the ratio of indirect expense incurred in a given period to direct labor cost, manufacturing cost, or another appropriate base for the same period. Final indirect cost rate means the indirect cost rate established and agreed upon by the government and the contractor as not subject to change.

Market Research: Collecting and analyzing information about capabilities within the market to satisfy agency needs.

Micro-purchase: An acquisition of supplies or services using simplified acquisition procedures, the aggregate amount of which does not exceed the micro-purchase threshold.

Micro-purchase Threshold: $3,000; except

a. $2,000 for acquisitions of construction subject to the Davis-Bacon Act,

b. $2,500 for acquisitions of services subject to the Service Contract Act; and

c. For acquisitions of supplies or services that, as determined by the head of the agency, are to be used to support a contingency operation or to facilitate defense against or recovery from nuclear, biological, chemical, or radiological attack, as described in 13.201(g)(1), except for construction subject to the Davis-Bacon Act (41 U.S.C. 428a)—

1. $15,000 in the case of any contract to be awarded and performed, or purchase to be made, inside the United States; and

2. $30,000 in the case of any contract to be awarded and performed, or purchase to be made, outside the United States. (FAR 2.101)

Nondevelopmental Items:

a. Any previously developed item of supply used exclusively for governmental purposes by a federal agency, a state or local government, or a foreign government with which the United States has a mutual defense cooperation agreement;

b. Any item described in paragraph (a) of this definition that requires only minor modification or modifications of a type customarily available in the commercial marketplace in order to meet the requirements of the procuring department or agency; or

c. Any item of supply being produced that does not meet the requirements of paragraph (a) or (b) of this definition solely because the item is not yet in use.

Offer: A response to a solicitation that, if accepted, would bind the offeror to perform the resultant contract. Responses to invitations for bids (sealed bidding) are offers called bids or sealed bids; responses to requests for proposals (negotiation) are offers called proposals. Responses to requests for quotations (simplified acquisition) are quotations, not offers.

Performance-based Acquisition: An acquisition structured around the results to be achieved as opposed to the manner by which the work is to be performed. (FAR 2.101)

Simplified Acquisition Threshold: $150,000. However, for acquisitions of supplies or services that, as determined by the head of the agency, are to be used to support a contingency operation or to facilitate defense against

or recovery from nuclear, biological, chemical, or radiological attack (41 U.S.C. 428a), the term means

a. $300,000 for any contract to be awarded and performed, or purchase to be made, inside the United States; and

b. $1 million for any contract to be awarded and performed, or purchase to be made, outside the United States. (FAR 2.101)

B. Definitions Clause (FAR 2.2)

A Definitions clause shall be inserted in any contract that exceeds the Simplified Acquisition Threshold.

FAR Part 3. Improper Business Practices and Personal Conflicts of Interest

A. Safeguards (FAR 3.1)

As a general rule, strictly avoid any conflict of interest or even the appearance of a conflict of interest in government–contractor relationships.

As a rule, no government employee may solicit or accept, directly or indirectly, any gratuity, gift, favor, entertainment, loan, or anything of monetary value from anyone who has or is seeking to obtain government business with the employee's agency, conducts activities that are regulated by the employee's agency, or has interests that may be substantially affected by the performance or nonperformance of the employee's official duties.

The Office of Federal Procurement Policy Act (41 U.S.C. 423), as amended, covers bribes, post-employment restrictions, obtaining and disclosing proprietary information, and other prohibited behaviors.

B. Contractor Gratuities To Government Personnel (FAR 3.2)

This provision requires that a clause prohibiting contractor gratuities be inserted in contracts above the simplified acquisition threshold and prescribes reporting and treatment of violations.

C. Reports Of Suspected Antitrust Violations (FAR 3.3)

Contracting personnel are an important source of investigative leads and information regarding antitrust violations, and they should be aware of any potential improper behavior by contractors and report any such behavior.

D. Contingent Fees (FAR 3.4)

This subpart prescribes the policies and procedures restricting the use of contingent fee arrangements to obtain federal contracts. A contingent fee is any commission, percentage, brokerage, or other fee that is contingent upon the success that a person or concern has in securing a government contract. It does not apply to commercial items or solicitations/contracts under the Simplified Acquisition Threshold (Part 13).

Contractors' arrangements to pay contingent fees for soliciting or obtaining government contracts have long been considered contrary to public policy because such arrangements may lead to attempted or actual exercise of improper influence. There are, however, certain exceptions such as payments to bona fide employees or bona fide agencies.

E. Other Improper Business Practices (FAR 3.5)

Buying-in, as used in this section, means submitting an offer below anticipated costs, expecting to

- Increase the contract amount after award (e.g., through unnecessary or excessively priced change orders); or

- Receive follow-on contracts at artificially high prices to recover losses incurred on the buy-in contract.

The government should minimize the opportunity for buying-in by seeking a price commitment covering as much of the entire program concerned as is practical by using multiyear contracting, with a requirement in the solicitation that a price be submitted only for the total multiyear quantity or priced options for additional quantities that, together with the firm contract quantity, equal the program requirements. Other safeguards are available to the contracting officer to preclude recovery of buying-in losses, (e.g., amortization of nonrecurring costs and treatment of unreasonable price quotations).

Kickback: Any money, fee, commission, credit, gift, gratuity, thing of value, or compensation of any kind that is provided, directly or indirectly, to any prime contractor, prime contractor employee, subcontractor, or subcontractor employee for the purpose of improperly obtaining or rewarding favorable treatment in connection with a prime contract or in connection with a subcontract relating to a prime contract. (FAR 3.502-1)

Subcontractor Kickbacks
The Anti-Kickback Act of 1986 (41 U.S.C. 51-58) was passed to deter subcontractors from making payments, and contractors from accepting payments, for the purpose of improperly obtaining or rewarding favorable treatment in connection with a prime contract or a subcontract relating to a prime contract. Anti-kickback requirements and restrictions on subcontractor sales to the government do not apply to commercial items or solicitations/contracts under the Simplified Acquisition Threshold. (Part 13).

F. Contracts with Government Employees or Organizations Owned or Controlled by Them (FAR 3.6)

Generally, a contracting officer shall not knowingly award any contract to a government employee or any organization owned or controlled by them. This policy is intended to avoid any conflict of interest and eliminate the appearance of favoritism.

G. Voiding and Rescinding Contracts (FAR 3.7)

This subpart describes policies and procedures for voiding and rescinding contracts in which an ethical violations has occurred, specifically:

- There has been a final conviction for bribery, conflict of interest, disclosure, or receipt of contractor bid or proposal information or source selection information in exchange for a thing of value, or to give anyone a competitive advantage in the award of a federal agency procurement contract, or similar misconduct; or

- There has been an agency head determination that contractor bid or proposal information or source selection information has been disclosed or received in exchange for a thing of value, or for the purpose of obtaining or giving anyone a competitive advantage in the award of a federal agency procurement contract.

H. Limitation on the Payment of Funds to Influence Federal Transactions (FAR 3.8)

In general, federal contract recipients are prohibited from using appropriated funds to pay any person for influencing or attempting to influence an officer or employee of any agency, a member of Congress, an officer or employee of Congress, or an employee of a member of Congress in connection with any covered federal actions. Specific exceptions and clarifications are detailed in this *FAR* clause.

I. Whistleblower Protections for Contractor Employees (FAR 3.9)

Government contractors are prohibited from discharging, demoting, or otherwise discriminating against an employee as a reprisal for disclosing information to a member of Congress, or an authorized official of an agency or of the Department of Justice, relating to a substantial violation of law related to a contract (including the competition for or negotiation of a contract). This subpart outlines specific complaint procedures, remedies, and enforcement.

J. Contractor Code of Business Ethics and Conduct (FAR 3.10)

This subpart prescribes policies and procedures for the establishment of contractor codes of business ethics and conduct, and display of agency Office of Inspector General (OIG) fraud hotline posters. Contractors should conduct themselves with the highest level of honesty and integrity and should have written policies governing conduct and ethics.

K. Preventing Personal Conflicts of Interest for Contractor Employees Performing Acquisition Functions (FAR 3.11)

The government's policy is to require contractors to both identify and prevent personal conflicts of interest of their covered employees; and prohibit covered employees who have access to non-public information by reason of performance on a government contract from using such information for personal gain.

For this section, a "covered employee" means an individual who performs an acquisition function closely associated with inherently governmental functions and is

- An employee of the contractor; or

- A subcontractor that is a self-employed individual treated as a covered employee of the contractor because there is no employer to whom such an individual could submit the required disclosures.

A "personal conflict of interest" is a situation in which a covered employee has a financial interest, personal activity, or relationship that could impair the employee's ability to act impartially and in the best interest of the government when performing under the contract. (A *de minimis* interest that would not "impair the employee's ability to act impartially and in the best interest of the government" is not covered under this definition.)

Among the sources of personal conflicts of interest are financial interests of the covered employee, of close family members, or of other members of the covered employee's household; other employment or financial relationships (including seeking or negotiating for prospective employment or business); and gifts, including travel. For example, financial interests may arise from

- Compensation, including wages, salaries, commissions, professional fees, or fees for business referrals;

- Consulting relationships (including commercial and technical advisory board memberships, or serving as an expert witness in litigation);

- Services provided in exchange for honorariums or travel expense reimbursements;

- Research funding or other forms of research support;

- Investment in the form of stock or bond ownership or partnership interest (excluding diversified mutual fund investments);

- Real estate investments;

- Patents, copyrights, and other intellectual property interests; or

- Business ownership and investment interests.

A. Contract Execution (FAR 4.1)

The contracting officer's name and official title shall be typed, stamped, or printed on the contract. The contracting officer normally signs the contract after it has been signed by the contractor. Only a contracting officer is authorized to sign a contract on behalf of the U.S. government.

The type of signatory for a contractor varies based on the type of corporate entity is involved. Four types of entities addressed specifically in this part include individuals, partnerships, corporations, and joint ventures.

Individual: A contract with an individual shall be signed by that individual.

Partnership: A contract with a partnership shall be signed in the partnership name.

Corporation: A contract with a corporation shall be signed in the corporate name, followed by the word "by" and the signature and title of the person authorized to sign. The contracting officer shall ensure that the person signing for the corporation has authority to bind the corporation.

Joint ventures: A contract with joint ventures may involve any combination of individuals, partnerships, or corporations.

B. Electronic Commerce in Contracting (FAR 4.5)

The federal government shall use electronic commerce whenever practicable or cost-effective. Before using electronic commerce, the agency head shall ensure that the agency systems are capable of ensuring authentication and confidentiality commensurate with the risk and magnitude of the harm from loss, misuse, or unauthorized access to or modification of the information. Agencies may accept electronic signatures and records in connection with government contracts. (FAR 4.502(c) and FAR 4.402(d))

C. Contract Reporting (FAR 4.6)

The Federal Procurement Data System (FPDS) provides a comprehensive Web-based tool for assembling, organizing, and presenting contract placement data for the federal government and can be accessed at **www.fpds.gov**. Federal agencies report data to the Federal Procurement Data Center (FPDC), which collects, processes, and disseminates official statistical data on federal contracting. All federal contact award data must be made public. Agencies must report the following contract actions over the micro-purchase threshold, regardless of solicitation process used, and agencies must report any modification to these contract actions that change previously reported contract action data, regardless of dollar value: definitive contract actions; indefinite delivery vehicles (task and delivery orders, GSA FSS, BPAs, BOAs); calls and orders awarded under indefinite delivery vehicles.

D. Contractor Record Retention (FAR Part 4.7)

Contractors must retain all records pertaining to a government contract for a minimum of three years from the date of final payment is made under the contract. Certain records specified in this part may be required to be kept for longer period.

E. Government Contract Files (FAR Part 4.8)

This subpart prescribes requirements for establishing, maintaining, and disposing of contract files. The documentation in the files should constitute a complete history of the transaction and provide a complete background as a basis for informed decisions, supporting actions taken during the term of the contract. In addition, it should provide necessary information for reviews, investigations, or potential litigation or congressional inquiries. These files can be maintained by various agencies in the manner that best achieves their purpose. These files are to be comprehensive, and a full listing of materials to be retained therein is contained in this subpart.

Specific requirements exist for the proper closeout of government contract files and the retention of information contained therein.

F. Central Contractor Registration (FAR Part 4.11)

This subpart prescribes policies and procedures for requiring contractor registration in the Central Contractor Registration (CCR) database, a part of the Business Partner Network (BPN) to both increase visibility of vendor sources (including their geographical locations) for specific supplies and services and establish a common source of vendor data for the government. Generally contractors must be registered in the CCR prior to contract award. Specific exceptions and guidance are contained within this subpart.

G. Representations and Certifications (FAR Part 4.12)

This subpart prescribes policies and procedures for requiring submission and maintenance of representations and certifications through the Online Representations and Certifications Application (ORCA) to eliminate the administrative burden for contractors of submitting the same information to various contracting offices and establish a common source for this information to procurement offices across the government. The ORCA is the one common source for contractors submitting and maintaining representations and certifications.

H. Personal Identity Verification (FAR Part 4.13)

Agencies must implement OMB guidance for personal identity verification for all affected contractor and subcontractor personnel when contract performance requires contractors to have routine physical access to a federally controlled facility and/or routine access to a federally controlled information system.

I. Reporting Executive Compensation and First-Tier Subcontract Awards (FAR 4.14)

Contractors are required to report subcontract award data and the total compensation of the five most highly compensated individuals of the contractor and subcontractor.

J. American Recovery and Reinvestment Act Reporting Requirements (FAR 4.15)

Contractors that receive awards (or modifications to existing awards) funded in whole or in part by the Recovery Act must report information including, but not limited to

- The dollar amount of contractor invoices;

- The supplies delivered and services performed;

- An assessment of the completion status of the work;

- An estimate of the number of jobs created and the number of jobs retained as a result of the Recovery Act funds;

- Names and total compensation of each of the five most highly compensated officers for the calendar year in which the contract is awarded; and

- Specific information on first-tier subcontractors.

FAR Part 5. Publicizing Contract Actions

A. Policy

Contract actions are to be publicized in order to increase competition, broaden industry participation in meeting government requirements, and assist small business concerns, small disadvantaged business concerns, and women-owned small business concerns in obtaining contracts and subcontracts. "Contract action," as used in this part, means an action resulting in a contract (including actions for additional supplies or services outside the existing contract scope), but does not include actions that are within the scope and under the terms of the existing contract (e.g., contract modifications issued pursuant to the Changes clause or funding and other administrative changes). (FAR 5.001)

For any requirement in the *FAR*, to publish a notice, the contracting officer must transmit the notice to the governmentwide point of entry (GPE).

B. Methods of Disseminating Information (FAR 5.1)

As required by the Small Business Act (15 U.S.C. 637(e)) and the Office of Federal Procurement Policy Act (41 U.S.C. 416), contracting officers must disseminate information on proposed contract actions as follows:

1. For proposed contract actions expected to exceed $25,000, by synopsizing in the GPE. (FAR 5.201)

2. For proposed contract actions expected to exceed $15,000, but not expected to exceed $25,000, by displaying in a public place, or by any appropriate electronic means, an unclassified notice of the

solicitation or a copy of the solicitation satisfying the requirements of 5.207(c). The notice must include a statement that all responsible sources may submit a response that, if timely received, must be considered by the agency. The information must be posted not later than the date the solicitation is issued, and must remain posted for at least 10 days or until after quotations have been opened, whichever is later.

C. Synopsis of Proposed Contract Actions (FAR 5.2)

Primary purposes of the GPE notice are to improve small business access to acquisition information and to enhance competition by identifying contracting and subcontracting opportunities. The GPE may be accessed at **www.fedbizopps.gov**.

FAR 5.202 lists exceptions to the synopsis requirement.

An agency must transmit a notice of proposed contract action to the GPE. (FAR 5.201) All publicizing and response times are calculated based on the date of publication. The publication date is the date the notice appears on the GPE. The notice must be published at least 15 days before issuance of a solicitation except that, for acquisitions of commercial items, the contracting officer may

- Establish a shorter period for issuance of the solicitation; or

- Use the combined synopsis and solicitation procedure. (FAR 12.603)

Contracting officers should consider the circumstances of the individual acquisition, such as the complexity, commerciality, availability, and urgency when establishing solicitation response times for either contract actions estimated to be greater than $25,000, but less than the simplified acquisition threshold or

contract actions for the acquisition of commercial items in an amount estimated to be greater than $25,000.

Except for the acquisition of commercial items, agencies shall allow at least 30 days response time for receipt of bids or proposals from the date of issuance of a solicitation, if the contract action is expected to exceed the simplified acquisition threshold.

Contracting officers may, unless they have evidence to the contrary, presume the notice was published one day after transmission to the GPE.

A prime contractor or subcontractor with a contract exceeding $150,000 with the opportunity to subcontract (for subcontractors the next tier contract must exceed $15,000) may publicize, via the GPE, subcontracting opportunities stemming from receipt of a government contract.

D. Synopses of Contract Awards (FAR 5.3)

Contracting officers must synopsize, through the GPE, awards exceeding $25,000 that are

- Covered by the World Trade Organization Government Procurement Agreement or a Free Trade Agreement (Subpart 25.4); or

- Likely to result in the award of any subcontracts.

However, the dollar threshold is not a prohibition against publicizing an award of a smaller amount when publicizing would be advantageous to industry or to the government.

Contracting officers shall release to the public and make information available on awards over $4 million.

E. Release of Information (FAR 5.4)

To preserve the integrity of the acquisition process, a high degree of business security must be maintained. Information relating to plans that would provide undue or discriminatory advantage to private or personal interests, received in confidence from an offeror, otherwise requiring protection under Freedom of Information Act or Privacy Act, or pertaining to internal agency communications, is not releasable.

To assist industry planning and to locate additional sources of supply, estimates of unclassified long-range acquisition requirements may be publicized if the information will assist industry in its planning and facilitate meeting the acquisition requirements, will not encourage undesirable practices, and will not indicate the existing or potential mobilization of the industry as a whole.

FAR Part 6.
Competition Requirements

A. Scope and Applicability (FAR 6.000 and 6.001)

This part prescribes policies and procedures, and provides for full and open competition, full and open competition after exclusion of sources, other than full and open competition, and competition advocates. This part applies to all acquisitions except

1. Contracts awarded using the simplified acquisition procedures of Part 13;

2. Contracts awarded using contracting procedures (other than those addressed in this part) that are expressly authorized by statute;

3. Contract modifications, including the exercise of priced options that were evaluated as part of the initial competition, that are within the scope and under the terms of an existing contract;

4. Orders placed under requirements contracts or definite-quantity contracts;

5. Orders placed under indefinite-quantity contracts that were entered into pursuant to this part when

   a. The contract was awarded under Subpart 6.1 or 6.2 and all responsible sources were realistically permitted to compete for the requirements contained in the order; or

   b. The contract was awarded under Subpart 6.3 and the required justification and approval adequately covers the requirements contained in the order; or

6. Orders placed against task order and delivery order contracts entered into pursuant to Subpart 16.5.

B. Full and Open Competition (FAR 6.1)

Full and open competition is the process by which all responsible sources are allowed to compete. Contracting officers are required, with certain limited exceptions (see FAR 6.2 and 6.3), to promote and provide for full and open competition in soliciting offers and awarding government contracts. Competitive procedures available for use in fulfilling the requirement for full and open competition are sealed bids, competitive proposals, combination of competitive procedures (e.g., two-step sealed bidding), and other competitive procedures (e.g., selection of sources for architect-engineer contracts).

C. Full and Open Competition after Exclusion of Sources (FAR 6.2)

Agencies may exclude sources if the agency head determines that to do so would increase or maintain competition and likely result in reduced overall costs; would be in the interest of national defense; would ensure the continuous availability of a reliable source of supplies or services; would satisfy projected needs based on a history of high demand; or satisfy a critical need for medical, safety, or emergency supplies. Every proposed contract action that falls under this provision must be supported by a D&F signed by the head of the agency or designee and not made on a class basis. (FAR 6.202(a)(1) through FAR 6.202(a)(6) and FAR 6.202(b)(1))

Set-asides for Small Business Concerns: To fulfill the statutory requirements relating to small business concerns, contracting officers may set aside solicitations to allow only such business concerns to compete. No separate justification or D&F is required under this part to set aside a contract action for small business concerns. (FAR 6.203)

Section 8(a) Competition: To fulfill the statutory requirements relating to section 8(a) of the Small Business Act, Contracting Officers may limit competition to eligible 8(a) contractors. No separate justification or D&F is required under this part to limit competition to eligible 8(a) contractors. (FAR 6.204)

Set-asides for HUBZone Small Business Concerns: To fulfill the statutory requirements relating to the HUBZone Act of 1997, contracting officers in participating agencies may set aside solicitations to allow only qualified HUBZone small business concerns to compete. No separate justification or D&F is required under this part to set aside a contract action for qualified HUBZone small business concerns.

Set-asides for Service-Disabled Veteran–Owned Small Business Concerns: To fulfill the statutory requirements relating to the Veterans Benefits Act of 2003, contracting officers may set aside solicitations to allow only service-disabled veteran-owned small businesses to compete. No separate justification or D&F is required under this part to set aside a contract action for service-disabled veteran-owned small businesses. (FAR 6.205(a) and FAR 6.205(b))

Set-asides for Economically Disadvantaged Women-Owned Small Business (EDWOSB) Concerns or Women-Owned Small Business (WOSB) Concerns: To fulfill the statutory requirements relating to 15 U.S.C. 637(m), Contracting Officers may set aside solicitations for only EDWOSB or WOSB concerns eligible under the WOSB program. No separate justification or D&F is required under this part to set aside a contract action for ED-WOSB concerns or WOSB concerns eligible under the WOSB program. (FAR 6.207)

Set-asides for Local Firms during a Major Disaster or Emergency: To fulfill the statutory requirements relating to 42.U.S.C. 5150, the Robert T. Stafford Disaster Relief and Emergency Assistance Act, contracting officers may set aside solicitations to allow only offerors residing or doing business primarily in the area affected by such major disaster or emergency to compete. No separate justification or D&F is required under this part to set aside a contract action. (FAR 6.208)

"Major disaster or emergency area" means the area included in the official presidential declaration(s) and any additional areas identified by the Department of Homeland Security.

D. Other Than Full and Open Competition (FAR 6.3)

Both 41 U.S.C. 253(c) and 10 U.S.C. 2304(c) authorize, under certain conditions, contracting without providing for full and open competition.

There are seven exceptions to full and open competition:

1. Only one responsible source,

2. Unusual and compelling urgency,

3. Industrial mobilization,

4. International agreement,

5. Source authorized or required by statute,

6. National security, and

7. Public interest.

The justification for other than full and open competition shall be approved in writing as follows:

- Contracts not exceeding $650,000 by the contracting officer;

- Contracts exceeding $650,000 but less than $12.5 million by the competition advocate;

- Contracts exceeding $12.5 million but not exceeding $62.5 million ($85.5 million for DOD, NASA, and Coast Guard); by the head of the procuring activity or a designee who is either a flag officer or GS-15; and

- Contracts exceeding this amount by the senior procurement executive of the agency.

The agency shall make publicly available the justifications required by this part.

E. Sealed Bidding and Competitive Proposals (FAR 6.4)

Sealed bids are appropriate when time permits; award will be made on the basis of price and other price-related factors, no discussions are required, and when there is reasonable expectation of receiving more than one bid. Competitive proposals are appropriate when sealed bids are not. Sealed bidding and competitive proposals are both acceptable procedures for use under full and open competition and full and open competition after exclusion of sources.

F. Competition Advocates (FAR 6.5)

Agency and procuring activity competition advocates are responsible for promoting the acquisition of commercial items; promoting full and open competition; challenging requirements that are not stated in terms of functions to be performed; performance required or essential physical characteristics; and challenging barriers to the acquisition of commercial items and full and open competition, such as unnecessarily restrictive statements of work, unnecessarily detailed specifications, and unnecessarily burdensome contract clauses.

FAR Part 7. Acquisition Planning

A. Acquisition Plans (FAR 7.1)

Acquisition planning is defined as the process by which the efforts of all personnel responsible for an acquisition are coordinated and integrated through a comprehensive plan for fulfilling the agency need in a timely manner and at a reasonable cost. Acquisition planning should begin as soon as the agency need is identified.

Acquisition planning and market research are required for all acquisitions to promote and provide for (a) acquisition of commercial items or, to the extent that commercial items suitable to the agency's needs are not available, nondevelopmental items, to the maximum extent practicable; (b) full and open competition or, when full and open competition is not required, obtaining competition to the maximum extent practicable; and (c) select the appropriate contract type in accordance with FAR Part 16.

The purpose of acquisition planning is to ensure that the government meets its needs in the most effective, economical, and timely manner. Acquisition planning should begin as soon as the agency need is identified, preferably well in advance of the fiscal year in which contract award or order placement is necessary. The acquisition team should consist of all those who will be responsible for significant aspects of the acquisition, such as contracting, fiscal, legal, and technical personnel. Early in the planning process, the planner should consult with requirements and logistics personnel who determine type, quality, quantity, and delivery requirements. If the plan proposes using other than full and open competition when awarding a contract, the plan shall also be coordinated with the cognizant competition advocate.

To facilitate attainment of the acquisition objectives, the plan must identify those milestones at which decisions should be made. The plan must address all technical, business, management, and other significant considerations that will control the acquisition. The specific content of plans will vary, depending on the nature, circumstances, and stage of the acquisition. In preparing the plan, the planner must follow the applicable instructions in paragraphs (a) and (b) of this section, together with the agency's implementing procedures. Acquisition plans for service contracts or orders must describe the strategies for implementing performance-based acquisition methods or must provide rationale for not using those methods. Contents of a written acquisition plan are addressed in FAR 7.105.

Bundling may provide substantial benefits to the government. However, because of the potential impact on small business participation, the head of the agency must conduct market research to determine whether bundling is necessary and justified. Market research may indicate that bundling is necessary and justified if an agency or the government would derive measurably substantial benefits.

B. Planning for the Purchase of Supplies in Economic Quantities (FAR 7.2)

Agencies are required by 10 U.S.C. 2384(a) and 41 U.S.C. 253(f) to procure supplies in such quantity as will result in the total cost and unit cost most advantageous to the government, where practicable, and will not exceed the quantity reasonably expected to be required by the agency. Solicitations for supplies, where practicable, will include a provision soliciting recommendations on economic order quantities.

C. Contractor Versus Government Performance

It is the policy of the government to perform inherently governmental activities with government personnel and subject commercial activities to the forces of competition.

D. Equipment Lease or Purchase (FAR 7.4)

FAR 7.401 delineates the factors that should be considered in making a lease vs. purchase decision.

Generally, the purchase method is appropriate if the equipment will be used beyond the point in time when cumulative leasing costs exceed the purchase costs. However, the lease method is appropriate if it is to the Government's advantage under the circumstances. If a lease is justified, a lease with option to purchase is preferable, but in this case, the contract shall state the purchase price or provide a formula that shows how the purchase price will be established at the time of purchase. Generally, a long-term lease should be avoided, but may be appropriate if an option to purchase or other favorable terms are included.

When requested by an agency, the General Services Administration (GSA) will assist in lease or purchase decisions by providing information such as pending price adjustments to Federal Supply Schedule contracts, recent or imminent technological developments, new techniques, and industry or market trends.

E. Inherently Governmental Functions (FAR 7.5)

Contracts shall not be used for the performance of inherently governmental functions. Agency decisions that determine whether a function is or is not an inherently governmental function may be reviewed and modified by appropriate Office of Management and Budget officials.

A representative list of inherently governmental functions is included within this subpart of the *FAR*. While the list is not exhaustive, it provides guidance into areas of work that are considered inherently governmental. Examples of this would include any criminal investigations or any prosecutions or adjudicary duties, with the exception of alternative dispute resolution. The command of any military forces is also inherently governmental, as are the conduct of foreign diplomacy or development of foreign policy or the performance of intelligence or counterintelligence. Issues relating to the federal workforce are also including in governmental functions, and that includes, hiring, job description development, and performance standards. Contractors are generally precluded from conducting any federal acquisition work and are not permitted to develop agency budget priorities, handle treasury funds (including collecting controlling or disbursing funds), distribute government property or make any determination relating to security clearances or eligibility for federal programs.

Contractors may perform a wide range of support to activities that are inherently governmental, but they must at all times be under the direct supervision and control of government employees.

Agency implementation of this subpart shall include procedures requiring the agency head or designated requirements official to provide the contracting officer, concurrent with transmittal of the statement of work (or any modification thereof), a written determination that none of the functions to be performed are inherently governmental. This assessment should place emphasis on the degree to which conditions and facts restrict the discretionary authority, decision-making responsibility, or accountability of government officials using contractor services or work products. Disagreements regarding the determination will be resolved in accordance with agency procedures before issuance of a solicitation.

FAR Part 8. Required Sources of Supplies and Services

This part deals with the acquisition of supplies and services from or through government supply sources.

Generally, agencies shall satisfy requirements for supplies and services from or through the sources and publications listed here in descending order of priority:

Supplies:
- Agency inventories;

- Excess from other agencies;

- Federal Prison Industries, Inc.;

- Supplies on the Procurement List maintained by the Committee for Purchase From People Who Are Blind or Severely Disabled;

- Wholesale supply sources, such as stock programs of the General Services Administration (GSA), Defense Logistics Agency, Department of Veterans Affairs, and military inventory control points;

- Mandatory Federal Supply Schedules;

- Optional use Federal Supply Schedules; and

- Commercial sources (including educational and nonprofit institutions).

Services:

- Services on the Procurement List maintained by the Committee for Purchase From People Who Are Blind or Severely Disabled;

- Mandatory Federal Supply Schedules;

- Optional use Federal Supply Schedules; and

- Federal Prison Industries, Inc. or commercial sources (including educational and nonprofit institutions).

A. Excess Personal Property (FAR 8.1)

Personal property is defined as property of any kind, or interest in it, except real property, records of the federal government, and the following categories of naval vessels—battleships, cruisers, aircraft carriers, destroyers, and submarines. When practicable, agencies must use excess personal property as the first source of supply for agency and cost-reimbursement contractor requirements. Agency personnel must make positive efforts to satisfy agency requirements by obtaining and using excess personal property (including that suitable for adaptation or substitution) before initiating a contract action.

B. Use of Federal Supply Schedules (FAR 8.4)

The Federal Supply Schedule program is also known as the GSA Schedules Program or the Multiple Award Schedule (MAS) Program. The program, directed and managed by the General Services Administration (GSA), provides federal agencies with a simplified process for obtaining commercial supplies and services at prices associated with volume buying. Indefinite delivery contracts are awarded to provide supplies and services at stated prices for given periods of time. The Department of Defense (DOD) manages similar systems of schedule-type contracting for military items; however, DOD systems are not covered by this subpart.

GSA offers two online tools to support using the program. GSA*Advantage!* is an online shopping service through which ordering activities may search specific information (i.e., national stock number, part number, common name), review delivery options, place orders directly with Schedule contractors, and pay for orders using the government-wide commercial purchase card. GSA's electronic request for quotation (RFQ) system, e-Buy, complements GSA*Advantage!* and allows ordering activities to post requirements, obtain quotes, and issue orders electronically.

For administrative convenience, an ordering activity contracting officer may add items not on the Federal Supply Schedule (also referred to as open market items) to a Federal Supply Schedule blanket purchase agreement (BPA) or an individual task or delivery order. The contracting officer must do the following:

- Follow all applicable acquisition regulations pertaining to the purchase of the items not on the Schedule (e.g., publicizing (Part 5), competition requirements (Part 6), acquisition of commercial items (Part 12), contracting methods (Parts 13, 14, and 15), and small business programs (Part 19));

- Determine the price for the items is fair and reasonable;

- Clearly label the items on the order as items not on the Federal Supply Schedule; and

- Include all contract clauses applicable to the items in the order.

Using Schedules (FAR 8.404)

FAR Parts 13 (except 13.303-2(c) (3)), 14, 15, and 19 (except for the requirement at 19.202-1(e) (1) (iii)) do not apply to BPAs or orders placed against Schedule contracts.

BPAs and orders placed against an MAS, using the procedures in this subpart, are considered to be issued using full and open competition. When establishing a BPA or placing orders under schedule contracts, ordering activities shall not seek competition outside of the Federal Supply Schedules or synopsize the requirement. Although the mandatory preference programs of Part 19 do not apply, orders placed against schedule contracts may be credited toward the ordering activity's small business goals.

Orders placed under a schedule contract must comply with:

- Acquisition planning requirements (FAR 7.1 and FAR Part 39);

- Requirements for a bundled contract (see 2.101(b)); and

- The requiring agency's statutory and regulatory requirements that apply to the supply or service.

GSA has already determined the prices of supplies and services under schedule contracts to be fair and reasonable. By placing an order against a schedule contract using the procedures in 8.405, the ordering activity has concluded that the order represents the best value and results in the lowest overall cost alternative (considering price, special features, administrative costs, etc.) to meet the government's needs. Although GSA has already negotiated fair and reasonable pricing, ordering activities may seek additional discounts before placing an order.

Ordering Procedures (FAR 8.405)

The ordering activity may seek a price reduction at any time. However, when an order exceeds the maximum order threshold, the ordering activity must seek a price reduction.

An order for supplies or services that are listed in the Schedules contracts at a fixed price for the performance of a specific task *does not require* a statement of work (e.g., installation, maintenance, and repair). An order for services priced at hourly rates as established by the Schedule *requires* a statement of work. To the maximum extent practicable, the agency requirements shall be performance-based statements.

The ordering activity shall evaluate all responses received using the evaluation criteria provided to the schedule contractors. The ordering activity is responsible for

- Considering the level of effort and the mix of labor proposed to perform a specific task being ordered;

- Determining that the total price is reasonable; and

- Placing the order, or establishing the BPA, with the schedule contractor that represents the best value. (FAR 8.404(d))

After award, ordering activities should provide timely notification to unsuccessful offerors.

Blanket Purchase Agreements (FAR 8.405-3)

Ordering activities may establish blanket purchase agreements (BPAs) under any schedule contract to fill repetitive needs for supplies or services. BPAs may be established with one or more schedule contractors. The number of BPAs to be established is within the discretion of the ordering activity establishing the BPAs and should be based on a strategy that is expected to maximize the effectiveness of the BPA(s) considering

- The scope and complexity of the requirement(s),

- The need to periodically compare multiple technical approaches or prices,

- The administrative costs of BPAs, and

- The technical qualifications of the schedule contractor(s).

If the ordering activity establishes one BPA, authorized users may place the order directly under the established BPA when the need for the supply or service arises. If the ordering activity establishes multiple BPAs, before placing an order exceeding the micro-purchase threshold, the ordering activity shall

- Forward the requirement, or statement of work and the evaluation criteria, to an appropriate additional number of BPA holders, as established in the BPA ordering procedures; and

- Evaluate the responses received, make a best value determination (see 8.404(d)), and place the order with the BPA holder that represents the best value.

If the BPA is for hourly rate services, the ordering activity shall develop a statement of work for requirements covered by the BPA. All orders under the BPA shall specify a price for the performance of the tasks identified in the statement of work.

BPAs generally should not exceed five years in length, but may do so to meet program requirements. Further, the ordering activity that establishes the BPA shall review it at least once a year to determine whether the schedule contract upon which the BPA was established is still in effect, the BPA still represents the best value, and the estimated quantities/amounts have been exceeded and additional price reductions can be obtained.

Limited Sources (FAR 8.405-6)

Orders placed under Federal Supply Schedules are exempt from the requirements in Part 6. However, when limiting competition by procuring an item under schedule from limited sources, the ordering activity must justify it in writing and obtain appropriate approvals. Conditions where this is required include orders or BPAs above the micro-purchase threshold, an order or BPA exceeding the simplified acquisition threshold, and an item peculiar to one manufacturer. An item peculiar to one manufacturer can be a particular brand name, product, or a feature of a product peculiar to one manufacturer. A brand name item, whether available on one or more schedule contracts, is an item peculiar to one manufacturer. Brand name specifications shall not be used unless the particular brand name, product, or feature is essential to the government's requirements, and market research indicates other companies' similar products, or products lacking the particular feature do not meet, or cannot be modified to meet, the agency's needs.

Ordering Activity Responsibilities (FAR 8.406)

Ordering activities are responsible for

- Order placement, and certain orders under certain conditions may be placed orally,

- Inspection and acceptance,

- Seeking appropriate remedies when the contractor delivers a supply or service that does not conform to the order requirements,

- Terminating individual orders for cause or convenience, and

- Issuing final decisions on disputes arising from performance of an order or referring the dispute to the schedule contracting officer.

Ordering activities must prepare an evaluation of contractor performance for each order that exceeds the simplified acquisition threshold IAW 42.1502(c).

C. Acquisition of Helium (FAR 8.5)

This section contains special requirements concerning this specialized procurement.

D. Acquisition from Federal Prison Industries, Inc. (FAR 8.6)

Federal Prison Industries, Inc. (FPI), also referred to as UNICOR, is a self-supporting, wholly owned government corporation of the District of Columbia. FPI provides training and employment for prisoners confined in federal penal and correctional institutions through the sale of its supplies and services to government agencies. FPI diversifies its supplies and services to prevent private industry from experiencing unfair competition from prison workshops or activities. Supplies manufactured and services performed by FPI are listed in the FPI Schedule, which can be accessed at **www.unicor.gov**.

FAR 8.604 discusses waivers for the use of the FPI Schedule. FAR 8.605 discusses when an exception to using the FPI may be appropriate, though purchase from FPI is not mandatory and a waiver may not be required.

E. Acquisition from Nonprofit Agencies Employing People who are Blind or Severely Disabled (FAR 8.7)

The National Industries for the Blind (NIB) and the National Industries for the Severely Handicapped (NISH) are central nonprofit agencies that were established under the Javits-Wagner-O'Day Act (JWOD). The JWOD Program has been rebranded as the AbilityOne Program, The Procurement List, a list of all supplies and services required to be purchased from AbilityOne participating nonprofit agencies, can be found online at www.abilityone.gov/procurementlist. Prices for supplies are normally adjusted semi-annually while the prices for services are normally adjusted annually.

The JWOD Act requires the government to purchase supplies or services on the Procurement List from AbilityOne participating nonprofit agencies if they are available within the period required. FPI and nonprofit agencies participating in the AbilityOne Program may produce identical supplies or services. When this occurs, ordering offices shall purchase supplies and services in the following order of priorities:

1. Supplies

   a. FPI

   b. AbilityOne participating nonprofit agencies

   c. Commercial sources

2. Services

   a. AbilityOne participating nonprofit agencies

   b. FPI or commercial sources

FAR 8.706 discusses exceptions to the use of AbilityOne agencies and the procedures to be followed to document such an exception.

FAR Part 9. Contractor Qualifications

A. Responsible Prospective Contractors (FAR 9.1)

Purchases are to be made from, and contracts awarded only to, responsible prospective contractors. To be determined responsible, a prospective contractor must

- Have adequate financial resources to perform the contract, or the ability to obtain them;

- Be able to comply with the required or proposed delivery or performance schedule, taking into consideration all existing commercial and governmental business commitments;

- Have a satisfactory performance record. Generally a prospective contractor shall not be determined responsible or nonresponsible solely on the basis of a lack of relevant performance history;

- Have a satisfactory record of integrity and business ethics;

- Have the necessary organization, experience, accounting and operational controls, and technical skills; or the ability to obtain them (including, as appropriate, such elements as production control procedures, property control systems, quality assurance measures, and safety programs applicable to materials to be produced or services to be performed by the prospective contractor and subcontractors);

- Have the necessary production, construction, and technical equipment and facilities, or the ability to obtain them; and

- Be otherwise qualified and eligible to receive an award under applicable laws and regulations. Note that there is a prohibition to contracting with an inverted domestic corporation at FAR 9.108. Inverted domestic corporation as used in this section, means a foreign incorporated entity treated as an inverted domestic corporation under 6 U.S.C.395(b), (i.e., a corporation that used to be incorporated in the United States or used to be a partnership in the United States but now is incorporated in a foreign country or is a subsidiary whose parent corporation is incorporated in a foreign country that meets the criteria specified in 6 U.S.C395(b) applied in accordance with the rules and definitions of 6 U.S.C. 395(c)).

A prospective contractor that is or recently has been seriously deficient in contract performance shall be presumed to be nonresponsible unless the contracting officer determines that the circumstances were properly beyond the contractor's control or that the contrac-

tor has taken appropriate corrective action. Past failure to apply sufficient tenacity and perseverance to perform acceptably is strong evidence of nonresponsibility. Failure to meet the quality requirements of the contract is a significant factor to consider in determining satisfactory performance. The CO shall consider the number of contracts involved and the extent of deficient performance in each contract when making this determination. If the pending contract requires a subcontracting plan pursuant to Subpart 19.7, the Small Business Subcontracting Program, the contracting officer shall also consider the prospective contractor's compliance with subcontracting plans under recent contracts in establishing that the prospective contractor has a satisfactory performance record.

When it is necessary for a particular acquisition or class of acquisition, the contracting officer shall develop (with the assistance of appropriate specialists) special standards of responsibility. Social standards may be particularly desirable when experience has demonstrated that unusual expertise or specialized facilities are needed for adequate contract performance. The special standards shall be set forth in the solicitation (and so identified) and shall apply to all offerors.

Contracting officers shall award contracts for subsistence only to those prospective contractors that meet the general standards in 9.104-1 and are approved in accordance with agency sanitation standards and procedures.

Upon making a determination of nonresponsibility with regard to a small business concern, the contracting officer shall refer the matter to the Small Business Administration, which will decide whether to issue a Certificate of Competency. (FAR 9.104-3(d))

Subcontractor Responsibility

Generally, prospective prime contractors are responsible for determining the responsibility of their prospective subcontractors (but see 9.405 and 9.405-2 regarding debarred, ineligible, or suspended firms). Determinations of prospective subcontractor responsibility may affect the government's determination of the prospective prime contractor's responsibility. A prospective contractor may be required to provide written evidence of a proposed subcontractor's responsibility. When it is the government's interest to do so, the contracting officer may directly determine a prospective subcontractor's responsibility. In this case, the same standards used to determine a prime contractor's responsibility shall be used by the government to determine subcontractor responsibility.

B. Qualifications Requirements (FAR 9.2)

Qualification requirement means a government requirement for testing or other quality assurance demonstration that must be completed before award of a contract. The activity responsible for establishment of the qualification requirements must periodically furnish through the government-wide point of entry (GPE) a notice seeking additional sources or products for qualification unless the contracting officer determines that such publication would compromise the national security.

Potential offerors need not be on a Qualified Bidders List, Qualified Manufacturers List, or Qualified Products List if they demonstrate they can meet the requirements before the specified award date.

C. First Article Testing and Approval (FAR 9.3)

First article testing and approval ensures that the contractor can furnish a product that conforms to all contract requirements for acceptance.

Before requiring first article testing and approval, the contracting officer must consider impact on cost or delivery, risk if not done, and availability of less costly methods of ensuring the desired quality.

Testing and approval may be appropriate when the contractor has not previously furnished the product to the government, or he or she has but there have been subsequent changes in processes or specifications, production has been discontinued, or the product was later found defective; the product is described by a performance specification; or it is essential to have an approved first article to serve as a manufacturing standard.

Normally, testing and approval is not required for research or development efforts, products requiring qualification before award, products normally sold in the commercial market, or products covered by complete and detailed technical specifications.

D. Debarment, Suspension, and Ineligibility (FAR 9.4)

Debarment means action taken by a debarring official to exclude a contractor from government contracting and government-approved subcontracting for a reasonable, specified period. Generally, debarment should not exceed three years, though exceptions to this are listed in FAR 9.406-4.

Suspension means action taken by a suspending official to disqualify a contractor temporarily from government contracting and government-approved subcontracting.

Ineligible means excluded from government contracting (and subcontracting, if appropriate) pursuant to statutory, executive order, or regulatory authority (other than the *FAR*).

Agencies are to solicit/award/consent to subcontract with responsible contractors only.

Debarment and suspension are discretionary actions that are imposed only in the public interest for the government's protection and not for the purposes of punishment.

Excluded Parties List System: GSA operates the web-based Excluded Parties List System (EPLS). The EPLS lists all contractors debarred, suspended, proposed for debarment, declared ineligible or excluded or disqualified under the nonprocurement common rule by agencies or by the Government Accountability Office. Each agency is responsible for updating EPLS, generally within five days after the action becomes effective or an action is modified or rescinded. After opening of bids or receipt of proposals, and immediately prior to award, the contracting officer shall review the list to ensure that the agency does not solicit offers, award contracts, or consent to subcontracts with contractors on the list.

Contractors debarred, suspended, or proposed for debarment are excluded from receiving contracts, and agencies shall not solicit offers from, award contracts to, or consent to subcontracts with these contractors, unless the agency head determines that there is a compelling reason for such action. Contractors shall not enter into any subcontract in excess of $30,000, other than a subcontract for a commercially available off-the-shelf item, with a contractor that has been debarred, suspended, or proposed for debarment unless there is a compelling reason to do so. If a contractor intends to subcontract, other than a subcontract for a commercially available off-the-shelf item, with a party that is debarred, suspended, or proposed for debarment as evidenced by the parties' inclusion in the EPLS, a corporate officer or designee of the contractor is required by operation of the clause at 52.209-4, "Protecting the Government's Interests when Subcontracting with Contractors Debarred, Suspended, or Proposed for Debarment," to notify the contracting officer in writing before entering into such contract.

Notwithstanding the debarment, suspension, or proposed debarment of a contractor, agen-cies may continue contracts or subcontracts in existence at the time the contractor was debarred, suspended, or proposed for debarment unless the agency head directs otherwise.

Causes for debarment are cited at FAR 9.406-2. FAR 9.407-2 lists causes for suspension. Period of debarment is cited in FAR 9.406-4. Scope of debarment is cited in FAR 9.406-5.

E. Organizational and Consultant Conflicts of Interest (FAR 9.5)

"Organizational conflict of interest" means that because of other activities or relationships with other persons, a person is unable or potentially unable to render impartial assistance or advice to the government, or the person's objectivity in performing the contract work is or might be otherwise impaired, or a person has an unfair competitive advantage.

This is most likely to occur in contracts for management support services; consultant or other professional services; contractor performance of, or assistance with, technical evaluations; or system engineering and technical direction by a contractor who does not have contractual responsibility.

Contracting officers must identify, avoid, neutralize, or mitigate organizational conflicts of interest.

F. Contractor Team Arrangements (FAR 9.6)

A contractor team arrangement is an arrangement in which two or more companies form a partnership or joint venture to act as a potential prime contractor; or a potential prime contractor agrees with one or more other companies to have them act as its subcontractors under a specified government contract or acquisition program. Contractor team arrangements may be desirable from both a government and industry standpoint to enable the companies involved to complement each other's unique capabilities and offer the government the best combination of performance, cost, and delivery for the system or product being acquired.

Contractor team arrangements may be particularly appropriate in complex research and development acquisitions, but may be used in other appropriate acquisitions, including production. The companies involved normally form a contractor team arrangement before submitting an offer. However, they may enter into an arrangement later in the acquisition process, including after contract award.

The government will recognize the integrity and validity of contractor team arrangements provided that the arrangements are identified and company relationships are fully disclosed in an offer or, for arrangements entered into after submission of an offer, before the arrangement becomes effective. The government will not normally require or encourage the dissolution of contractor team arrangements.

G. Defense Production Pools and Research and Development Pools (FAR 9.7)

A pool shall be treated the same as any other prospective or actual contractor except as stated below. The contracting officer shall not award a contract to a pool unless the offer leading to the contract is submitted by the pool in its own name or by an individual pool member expressly stating that the offer is on behalf of the pool. Upon receipt of an offer submitted by a group representing that it is a pool, the contracting officer shall verify its approved status with the SBA District Office Director or other approving agency and document the contract file that the verification was made. Pools approved by the SBA under the Small Business Act are entitled to the preferences and privileges accorded to small business concerns. Approval under the Defense Production Act does not confer these preferences and privileges. Before awarding a contract to

an unincorporated pool, the contracting officer shall require each pool member participating in the contract to furnish a certified copy of a power of attorney identifying the agent authorized to sign the offer or contract on that member's behalf.

Pool members may submit individual offers, independent of the pool. However, the contracting officer shall not consider an independent offer by a pool member if that pool member participates in a competing offer submitted by the pool. If a pool member submits an individual offer, independent of the pool, the contracting officer shall consider the pool agreement, along with other factors, in determining whether that pool member is a responsible prospective contractor.

FAR Part 16. Types of Contracts

A. Selecting Contract Types (FAR 16.1)

Contract types vary according to the degree and timing of the responsibility assumed by the contractor for the costs of performance and the amount and nature of the profit incentive offered to the contractor for achieving or exceeding goals. Contract types are grouped into two broad categories: fixed price and cost reimbursement.

Selecting the contract type is generally a matter for negotiation and requires the exercise of sound judgment. Negotiating the contract type and negotiating prices are closely related and should be considered together. The objective is to negotiate a contract type and price (or estimated cost and fee) that will result in reasonable contractor risk and provide the contractor with the greatest incentive for efficient and economical performance. A firm-fixed-price contract, which best utilizes the basic profit motive of business enterprise, shall be used when the risk involved is minimal or can be predicted with an acceptable degree of certainty. However, when a reasonable basis for firm pricing does not exist, other contract types should be considered, and negotiations should be directed toward selecting a contract type (or combination of types) that will appropriately tie profit to contractor performance.

In the course of an acquisition program, a series of contracts, or a single long-term contract, changing circumstances may make a different contract type appropriate in later periods than that used at the outset. In particular, contracting officers should avoid protracted use of a cost-reimbursement or time-and-materials contract after experience provides a basis for firmer pricing.

Factors that should be considered in selecting contract type are delineated in FAR 16.104. These include price competition and analysis, cost analysis, type and complexity of the requirement, and its urgency. Several factors regarding the contractor also influence contract type, such as the contractor's accounting system and ability to account for a complex contract, technical capability, and financial responsibility. All considerations should be fully considered and documented in the contract file.

B. Fixed-Price Contracts (FAR 16.2)

Firm-fixed-price contracts provide for a price that is not subject to any adjustment on the basis of the contractor's cost experience in performing the contract. This contract type places upon the contractor maximum risk and full responsibility for all costs and resulting profit or loss. It provides maximum incentive for the contractor to control costs and perform effectively and imposes a minimum administrative burden upon the contracting parties. The contracting officer may use a firm-fixed-price contract in conjunction with an award-fee incentive (FAR 16.404) and performance or delivery incentives (FAR 16.402-2 and 16.402-3) when the award fee or incentive is based solely on factors other than cost. The contract type remains firm-fixed-price when used with these incentives.

A firm-fixed-price contract is suitable for acquiring commercial items (see Parts 2 and 12) or for acquiring other supplies or services on the basis of reasonably definite functional or detailed specifications (see Part 11) when the contracting officer can establish fair and reasonable prices at the outset, such as when

1. There is adequate price competition;

2. There are reasonable price comparisons with prior purchases of the same or similar supplies or services made on a competitive basis or supported by valid cost or pricing data;

3. Available cost or pricing information permits realistic estimates of the probable costs of performance; or

4. Performance uncertainties can be identified and reasonable estimates of their cost impact can be made, and the contractor is willing to accept a firm fixed price representing assumption of the risks involved.

Fixed-price incentive contracts are fixed-price contracts that provide for the adjustment of profit and establishment of the final contract price by a formula based on the relationship of final negotiated total cost to total target cost. This contract type is appropriate for development and production efforts.

Fixed-price with economic price adjustment provides for upward or downward revision of the stated contract price upon occurrence of specified contingencies. Economic price adjustments can be based on established prices, actual costs of labor or material, or cost indexes of labor or material. This contract type is appropriate when there is serious doubt concerning the future stability of market or labor conditions over an extended period of contract performance, and when contingencies that would otherwise be included in the contract price can be identified and covered separately.

Fixed-price with prospective price redetermination results in a firm-fixed-price for an initial period with prospective redetermination at a stated time during performance. Appropriate for production or services for which it is possible to negotiate a fair and reasonable firm fixed price for an initial period, but not for subsequent periods of contract performance.

Fixed ceiling price with retroactive price redetermination provides for a fixed ceiling price and price redetermination within the ceiling after contractor completion. Appropriate for research and development efforts valued at $150,000 or less.

A *Firm-fixed-price/level-of-effort term contract* requires the contractor to provide a specified level of effort over a stated period of time for work that can only be stated in general terms, and requires the government to pay a fixed dollar amount for these services. Appropriate for investigation or study in a specific research and development area.

Time-and-materials contracts and labor-hour contracts are not fixed-priced contracts.

C. Cost Reimbursement Contracts (FAR 16.3)

A *cost reimbursement contract* provides for payment of allowable incurred costs, to the extent prescribed in the contract. They are suitable when uncertainties involved in contract performance do not permit costs to be estimated with sufficient accuracy to use any type of fixed-price contract. The contracting officer shall use cost reimbursement contracts only when circumstances do not allow the agency to define its requirements sufficiently to allow for a fixed-price type contract or uncertainties involved in contract performance do not permit costs to be estimated with sufficient accuracy to use any type of fixed-price contract. The contracting officer shall document the rationale for selecting the contract type in the written acquisition plan and

ensure that the plan is approved and signed by at least one level above the contracting officer. The use of a cost reimbursement–type contract requires that the contractor's accounting system be adequate for determining costs applicable to the contract and that adequate government resources are available to award and manage a contract other than firm-fixed-price. They may not be used to acquire commercial items.

A *cost contract* is a cost reimbursement contract in which the contractor receives no fee. These may be appropriate for research and development work, particularly with nonprofit educational institutions or other nonprofit organizations.

A *cost-plus-incentive-fee contract* provides for an initially negotiated fee to be adjusted later by a formula based on the relationship of total allowable costs to total target costs. Appropriate for services or development and test programs, as well as others if use of both cost and technical performance incentives is desired and administratively practical.

A *cost-plus-award-fee contract* provides for a fee consisting of a base amount (which may be zero) fixed at inception of the contract and an award amount, based upon a judgmental evaluation by the government, sufficient to provide motivation for excellence in contract performance. They are costly to administer and appropriate for level of effort services that can only be subjectively measured.

A *cost-plus-fixed-fee contract* provides for payment of a negotiated fee that is fixed at the inception of the contract and that does not vary with actual costs incurred, though it may be adjusted as a result of changes in the work to be performed under the contract. There are two types: completion form (clearly defined task with a definite goal and specific end product) and term form (scope of work described in general terms). Completion form is preferred. This contract type is costly to administer and is the least preferred type because the contractor assumes no financial risk. Appropriate for research and development.

D. Incentive Contracts (FAR 16.4)

Incentive contracts are appropriate when a firm-fixed-price contract is not appropriate and the required supplies/services can be acquired at lower costs and, in certain instances, with improved delivery or technical performance by relating the amount of profit or fee payable to the contractor's performance. Incentives can be applied to cost, technical performance, and/or delivery.

A *fixed-price incentive contract* is a fixed-price contract that provides for adjustment of profit and establishment of the final contract price by applying a formula based on the relationship of total final negotiated cost to total target cost. There are two forms: firm target— firm target cost, target profit, and profit sharing formula negotiated into basic contract, with profit adjusted upon contract completion; and successive targets—initial cost and profit targets negotiated into contract but final cost target (firm) not negotiated until sometime during performance. Appropriate for development and production.

A *fixed-price contract with an award fee* is appropriate when the government wishes to motivate a contractor and other incentives cannot be used because contractor performance cannot be measured objectively. Such contracts include a fixed price (including normal profit) for the effort. This price is paid for satisfactory performance. Award fee earned (if any) is paid in addition to that fixed price. This contract type is appropriate when the administrative cost of conducting award-fee evaluations are not expected to exceed the expected benefits; procedures have been established for conducting the award-fee evaluation; the award-fee board has been established; and an individual above the level of the contracting officer approved the fixed-price-award-fee incentive.

There are two forms of cost-reimbursement incentive contracts: cost-plus-incentive-fee and cost-plus-award-fee (reference paragraph c).

E. Indefinite-Delivery Contracts (FAR 16.5)

Indefinite-delivery contracts are appropriate when the exact times and/or quantities of future deliveries are not known at the time of contract award. There are three types:

A *definite-quantity contract* provides for delivery of a definite quantity of specific supplies or services for a fixed period, with deliveries or performance to be scheduled at designated locations upon order. It is appropriate when it can be determined in advance that a definite quantity of supplies or services will be required during the contract period and the supplies or services are regularly available or will be available after a short lead-time.

A *requirements contract* provides for acquisition of all actual purchase requirements of designated government activities for specific supplies or services during a specified period of time, with deliveries or performance to be scheduled by placing orders. It is appropriate for acquiring supplies or services when the government anticipates recurring requirements but cannot predetermine the precise quantities of supplies or services that designated government activities will need during a definite period.

An *indefinite-quantity contract* provides for an indefinite quantity, within stated limits, of specific supplies or services to be furnished during a fixed period, with deliveries or performance to be scheduled by placing orders. Quantity limits may be expressed in terms of numbers of units or as dollar values. The contract shall require the government to order and the contractor to furnish at least a stated minimum quantity of supplies or services. In addition, if ordered, the contractor shall furnish any additional quantities, not to exceed the stated maximum. The contracting officer should use an indefinite-quantity contract only when a recurring need is anticipated. The government prefers to make multiple awards. The contracting officer must, to the maximum extent practicable, give preference to making multiple awards under a single solicitation for the same or similar supplies or services to two or more sources. (Exception: indefinite-quantity contracts for advisory and assistance services).

The contracting officer must provide each awardee a fair opportunity to be considered for each order exceeding $3,000 issued under multiple delivery-order contracts or multiple task-order contracts. Exceptions include:

1. Urgency of need results in an unacceptable delay;

2. Only one awardee is capable of performing;

3. The order must be issued on a sole-source basis in the interest of economy and efficiency as a logical follow-on to an order already issued under the contract;

4. It is necessary to place an order to satisfy a minimum guarantee;

5. For orders exceeding the simplified acquisition threshold a statute expressly authorizes or requires that the purchase be made from a specified source; and

6. In accordance with section 1331 of Public Law 111-240 (15 U.S.C. 644(r)), contracting officers may, at their discretion, set aside orders for any of the small business concerns identified in 19.000(a)(3). When setting aside orders for small business concerns, the specific small business program eligibility requirements identified in Part 19 apply.

Orders placed under a task-order contract or delivery-order contract awarded by another agency (i.e., a governmentwide acquisition contract or multi-agency contract) are not exempt from developing acquisition plans (see Subpart 7.1), and an information technology acquisition strategy (see Part 39). In addition, placing such orders may not be used to circumvent conditions and limitations imposed on the use of funds (e.g., 31 U.S.C. 1501(a)(1)).

F. Time-and-Materials, Labor-Hour, and Letter Contracts (FAR 16.6)

Time and materials contracts provide for acquiring supplies/services on the basis of direct labor hours at specified fixed hourly rates that include wages, overhead, profit, and materials (at cost). They may be used only when it is not possible at the time of placing the contract to estimate accurately the extent or duration of the work or to anticipate costs with any reasonable degree of confidence. Appropriate for engineering and design services.

Labor-hour contracts are a type of time and material contract differing only in that materials are not furnished by the contractor (often used in conjunction with other contract types).

Letter contracts are written, preliminary contractual instruments that authorize the contractor to begin immediately manufacturing supplies or performing services. They must include price ceiling ("not to exceed") and milestones for definitization. Appropriate only when the government's interests demand that the contractor be given a binding commitment so that work can commence immediately and it is not possible to negotiate a definitive contract in sufficient time. It must be superseded by definitized contract at the earliest possible date.

G. Agreements (FAR 16.7)

A *basic agreement* is a written instrument of understanding that contains contract clauses applying to future contracts between the parties during its term and contemplates separate future contracts that will incorporate by reference or attachment the required and applicable clauses agreed upon in the basic agreement. They are not contracts.

Basic ordering agreements are written instruments of understanding that contain terms and conditions which apply to future orders, a description of supplies and services to be provided, and methods for pricing, issuing, and delivering future orders under the basic ordering agreement. They are not contracts.

FAR Part 17. Special Contracting Methods

This part prescribes policies and procedures for the acquisition of supplies and services through special contracting methods, including multi-year contracting, options, and leader company contracting.

A. Multi-Year Contracting (FAR 17.1)

Multi-year contracting is a special contracting method to acquire known requirements in quantities and total cost not over planned requirements for up to five years unless otherwise authorized by statute, even though the total funds ultimately to be obligated may not be available at the time of contract award. This method may be used in sealed bidding or contracting by negotiation.

Using multi-year contracting is encouraged to take advantage of one or more of the following: lower costs; enhancing standardization; reducing administrative burden in placing and administering contracts; substantial continuity of production or performance, thus avoiding annual startup costs, preproduction testing costs, make-ready expenses, and phase-out costs; stabilizing contractor work forces; avoiding the need for establishing quality control techniques and procedures for a new contractor each year; broadening the competitive base with opportunity for participation

by firms not otherwise willing or able to compete for lesser quantities, particularly in cases involving high startup costs; and providing incentives to contractors to improve productivity through investment in capital facilities, equipment, and advanced technology.

B. Options (FAR 17.2)

An option is a unilateral right in a contract by which, for a specified period of time, the government may elect to purchase additional supplies/services called for in the contract, or may elect to extend the term of the contract. Generally, contracting officers must ensure contract options do not extend beyond five years for services, excluding IT services.

Inclusion of options is normally not in the government's interest when foreseeable requirements involve minimum economic quantities; delivery requirements are far enough into the future to permit competitive acquisition, production, and delivery; or an indefinite quantity or requirements contract would be more appropriate than a contract with options.

Contracts may express options for increased quantities of supplies or services in terms of a percentage of specific line items, an increase in specific line items, or additional numbered line items identified as the option. Contracts may express extensions of the term of the contract as an amended completion date or as additional time for performance (e.g., days, weeks, or months).

Options may be exercised within the time period specified in the contract only after it is determined that funds are available; the contractor is not on the Excluded Parties List; the requirement covered by the option fulfills an existing government need; exercise of the option is the most advantageous method of fulfilling the government's needs, price, and other factors considered; and the option was synopsized in accordance with FAR Part 5.

C. Leader Company Contracting (FAR Part 17.4)

Leader company contracting is an extraordinary acquisition technique that is limited to special circumstances and used only when in accordance with agency procedures. A developer or sole producer of a product or system is designated under this acquisition technique to be the leader company, and to furnish assistance and know-how under an approved contract to one or more designated follower companies, so they can become a source of supply. The objectives of this technique are one or more of the following:

- Reduce delivery time;

- Achieve geographic dispersion of suppliers;

- Maximize the use of scarce tooling or special equipment;

- Achieve economies in production;

- Ensure uniformity and reliability in equipment, compatibility or standardization of components, and interchangeability of parts;

- Eliminate problems in the use of proprietary data that cannot be resolved by more satisfactory solutions; or

- Facilitate the transition from development to production and to subsequent competitive acquisition of end items or major components.

Leader company contracting is to be used only when

1. The leader company has the necessary production know-how and is able to furnish required assistance to the follower(s);

2. No other souce can meet the Government's requirements without the assistance of a leader company;

3. The assistance required of the leader company is limited to that which is essential to enable the follower(s) to produce the items; and

4. Its use is authorized in accordance with agency procedures.

When leader company contracting is used, the government shall reserve the right to approve subcontracts between the leader company and the follower(s).

D. Interagency Acquisition (FAR Part 17.5)

Interagency acquisitions are commonly conducted through indefinite-delivery contracts, such as task- and delivery-order contracts. The indefinite-delivery contracts used most frequently to support interagency acquisitions are Federal Supply Schedules (FSS), governmentwide acquisition contracts (GWACs), and multi-agency contracts (MACs). An agency shall not use an interagency acquisition to circumvent conditions and limitations imposed on the use of funds.

Interagency acquisition may be accomplished through either assisted or direct acquisitions.

Assisted acquisitions: Prior to requesting that another agency conduct an acquisition on its behalf, the requesting agency shall make a determination that the use of an interagency acquisition represents the best procurement approach. As part of the best procurement approach determination, the requesting agency shall obtain the concurrence of the requesting agency's responsible contracting office in accordance with internal agency procedures. At a minimum, the determination shall include an analysis of procurement approaches, including an evaluation by the requesting agency that using the acquisition services of another agency achieves the following:

- Satisfies the requesting agency's schedule, performance, and delivery requirements (taking into account factors such as the servicing agency's authority, experience, and expertise as well as customer satisfaction with the servicing agency's past performance);

- Is cost effective (taking into account the reasonableness of the servicing agency's fees); and

- Will result in the use of funds in accordance with appropriation limitations and compliance with the requesting agency's laws and policies.

Direct acquisitions: Prior to placing an order against another agency's indefinite-delivery vehicle, the requesting agency shall make a determination that use of another agency's contract vehicle is the best procurement approach and shall obtain the concurrence of the requesting agency's responsible contracting office. At a minimum, the determination shall include an analysis, including the following factors:

- The suitability of the contract vehicle;

- The value of using the contract vehicle, including the administrative cost savings from using an existing contract and lower prices, greater number of vendors, and reasonable vehicle access fees; and

- The expertise of the requesting agency to place orders and administer them against the selected contract vehicle throughout the acquisition lifecycle.

E. Management and Operating Contracts (FAR Part 17.6)

Management and operating contracts are agreements under which the government contracts for the operation, maintenance, or support on its behalf of a government-owned-or-controlled research, development, special production, or testing establishment wholly or principally devoted to one or more major programs of the contracting federal agency.

A management and operating contract is characterized both by its purpose and by the special relationship it creates between government and contractor. The following criteria can generally be applied in identifying management and operating contracts:

1. Government-owned-or-controlled facilities must be utilized; for instance,

    o In the interest of national defense or mobilization readiness;

    o To perform the agency's mission adequately; or

    o Because private enterprise is unable or unwilling to use its own facilities for the work.

2. Because of the nature of the work, or because it is to be performed in government facilities, the government must maintain a special, close relationship with the contractor and the contractor's personnel in various important areas (e.g., safety, security, cost control, site conditions).

3. The conduct of the work is wholly or at least substantially separate from the contractor's other business, if any.

4. The work is closely related to the agency's mission and is of a long-term or continuing nature, and there is a need

    o To ensure its continuity, and

    o For special protection covering the orderly transition of personnel and work in the event of a change in contractors.

Effective work performance under management and operating contracts usually involves high levels of expertise and continuity of operations and personnel. Because of program requirements and the unusual (sometimes unique) nature of the work performed under management and operating contracts, the government is often limited in its ability to effect competition or to replace a contractor. Therefore, contracting officers should take extraordinary steps before award to assure themselves that the prospective contractor's technical and managerial capacity are sufficient, that organizational conflicts of interest are adequately covered, and that the contract will grant the government broad and continuing rights to involve itself, if necessary, in technical and managerial decision-making concerning performance.

FAR Part 18. Emergency Acquisitions

This section of the *FAR* provides a consolidated listing of flexibilities that are available for emergency acquisitions. These acquisition flexibilities are NOT exempt from the requirements and limitations stemming from FAR Part 3 (Improper Business Practices and Personal Conflicts of Interests). These flexibilities are specific techniques or procedures that may be used to streamline the standard acquisition process and include generally available flexibilities and emergency acquisition flexibilities that are available only under prescribed circumstances.

A. Available Acquisition Flexibilities (FAR 18.1)

This subpart summarizes a variety of acquisition flexibilities established elsewhere in the *FAR*. The *FAR* includes many acquisition flexibilities that are available to the contracting officer when certain conditions are met. These acquisition flexibilities do not require an emergency declaration or designation of contingency operation.

- Central Contractor Registry (CCR) registration is not required for contractors for an emergency acquisition. However, only contractors registered in the CCR may access the Disaster Response Registry. (FAR 26.205)

- Contracting officers do not have to synopsize a requirement if there is an unusual and compelling urgency and the government would be seriously injured by complying with the notice time periods. (FAR 5.202(a)(2))

- Agencies may limit sources and/or full and open competition when the requirement is urgent. (FAR 6.302-2)

- Contracting officers may take advantage of pre-existing Federal Supply Schedules, multi-agency blanket purchase agreements, and multi-agency indefinite delivery contracts to streamline the contracting process. (FAR 8.405-3(a)(6) and 16.505(a)(7))

- Federal Prison Industries is not considered a required source when public exigency requires immediate performance. (FAR 8.605(b))

- Contracting officers need not comply with the requirement for 90-day advance notification to AbilityOne when specifications or requirements are changed for emergency needs. (FAR 8.712(d))

- Agencies may relax or not enforce qualification requirements when an emergency exists. (FAR 9.206-1)

- Agencies may make use of the Defense Priorities and Allocations System (DPAS), as appropriate. (FAR 11.6)

- When under the simplified acquisition threshold, contracting officers may solicit from a single source under certain circumstances. (FAR 13.106-1(b))

- Contracting officers may utilize both oral requests for proposals and letter contracts. (FAR 15.203(f) and 16.603)

- Agencies may employ interagency acquisition. (FAR 17.5)

- Agencies may take advantage of streamlined small business programs, including 8(a) awards and sole-source awards to Historically Underutilized Business Zone (HUBZone) or Service-Disabled–Veteran-Owned small business concerns. (FAR 19.8, 19.1306, 19.1406, and 19.15)

- Contracting officers may retroactively approve overtime. (FAR 22.103-4(i))

- Certain requirements related to trade agreements are waived when contracts are awarded without full and open competition. (FAR 25.401(a)(5))

- The requirement to obtain prior authorization for use of patented technology may be waived. (FAR 27.204-1)

- The chief of the contracting office may waive the requirement for obtaining bid guarantees when performance and/or payment bonds are required. (FAR 28.101-1(c))

- Agencies may use the authority of Public Law 85-804 (concerning extraordinary contractual actions) to authorize advance payments to facilitate national defense. (FAR 32.405)

- Certain aspects to the assignment of claims policy may be relaxed. (FAR 32.803(d))

- The requirement to use electronic funds transfer as the method of payment may be waived. (FAR 32.1103(e))

- In the presence of urgent and compelling circumstances, the head of contracting activity may override protest procedures of the Government Accountability Office. (FAR 33.104(b) and (c))

- Under certain programs approved by the Federal Emergency Management Agency, the use of government property by contractors free of rent may be approved in certain circumstances. (FAR 45.301)

- Public Law 85-804 authorizes extraordinary contractual actions to facilitate the national defense, including the modification of contracts without consideration, correcting or mitigating mistakes in a contract, and formalizing informal commitments. (FAR 50.1)

B. Emergency Acquisition Flexibilities (FAR 18.2)

This subpart summarizes additional acquisition flexibilities that relate to the method of acquisition.

Per FAR 2.101, a contingency operation is defined as a military operation that

1. Is designated by the Secretary of Defense as an operation in which members of the armed forces are or may become involved in military actions, operations, or hostilities against an enemy of the United States or against an opposing military force; or

2. Results in the call or order to, or retention of, active duty of members of the uniformed services under section 688, 12301(a), 12302, 12304, 12305, or 12406 of 10 U.S.C., Chapter 15 of 10 U.S.C., or any other provision of law during a war or during a national emergency declared by the president or Congress.

When the agency head determines that supplies or services are being procured in support of a contingency operation, micro-purchase procedures may be used for requirements up to $15,000 for contracts awarded and performed, or purchase made, in the United States. For requirements awarded and performed, or purchase made, outside the United States, micro-purchase procedures may be used if the contract will not exceed $30,000. (FAR 13.201(g)) The same higher thresholds apply for purchase made in defense against or recovery from nuclear, biological, chemical, or radiological attack.

When the agency head determines that supplies or services are being procured in support of a contingency operation, simplified acquisition procedures may be used for requirements up to $300,000 for contracts awarded and performed, or purchase made, in the United States. For requirements awarded and performed, or purchase made, outside the United States, simplified acquisition procedures may be used if the contract will not exceed $1,000,000. (FAR 2.101) The same higher thresholds apply for purchase made in defense against or recovery from nuclear, biological, chemical, or radiological attack.

In support of a contingency operation, agencies may elect to use the SF-44 (purchase order-invoice-voucher) for contracts exceeding the micro-purchase threshold. (FAR 13.306)

When the president has made a declaration of an emergency or major disaster under the Robert T. Stafford Disaster Relief and Emergency Assistance Act, preference will be given to local contractors either through a local area set-aside or an evaluation preference. (FAR 6.208 and 26.2)

Section

TWO

FAR Parts 10–12

This section of the *FAR* outlines policies and procedures for conducting market research. This ensures that the government uses the most appropriate approach to acquiring, distributing, and supporting supplies and services.

A. Policy (FAR 10.001)

Agencies must ensure that legitimate needs are identified and tradeoffs evaluated to acquire items that meet those needs.

The agency must also conduct market research appropriate to the circumstances before it develops new requirements documents and before soliciting offers in most circumstances. Agencies shall conduct market research on an ongoing basis, and take advantage of commercially available market research methods to identify the capabilities (including the capabilities of small businesses and new entrants into federal contracting) that are available in the marketplace for meeting the requirements of the agency in furtherance of defense against or recovery from terrorism or nuclear, biological, chemical, or radiological attack.

Market research is done to determine if sources capable of satisfying the agency's requirements exist and to determine the extent to which commercial items or nondevelopmental items could either meet the need or could be incorporated at any point of the manufacturing process to reduce costs or increase energy efficiency or the use of recovered materials.

The requests for information made as part of market research should not be unduly burdensome.

If the agency anticipates bundling a contract at any point it should consult with the SBA procurement center representative and notify any incumbent small business that would be impacted by the bundling.

B. Procedures (FAR 10.002)

Market research is conducted to determine if commercial or non-developmental items are available to meet the government's needs or could be modified to meet them. The extent thereof will vary, depending on such factors as urgency, estimated dollar value, complexity, and past experience. Techniques for conducting market research include the following:

- Contacting knowledgeable individuals in government and industry regarding market capabilities to meet requirements;

- Reviewing the results of recent market research undertaken to meet similar or identical requirements;

- Publishing formal requests for information;

- Querying government databases that provide information relevant to agency acquisitions;

- Communicating online with industry, acquisition personnel, and customers;

- Obtaining source lists of similar items from other contracting activities or agencies;

- Reviewing catalogs and other generally available product literature published by manufacturers, distributors, and dealers or available online; and

- Conducting interchange meetings or holding presolicitation conferences.

If market research indicates commercial or nondevelopmental items might not be available to satisfy agency needs, agencies are required to reevaluate the need and determine whether the need can be restated to permit commercial or nondevelopmental items to satisfy their need.

If market research establishes that the government's need may be met by a type of item or service customarily available in the commercial marketplace that would meet the definition of a commercial item, the contracting officer must solicit and award any resultant contract in accordance with FAR Part 12.

If market research establishes that the government's need cannot be met by a type of item or service customarily available in the marketplace, FAR Part 12 shall not be used.

Similar obligations exist for prime contractors. Under prime contracts greater than $5 million for other than commercial items, before awarding any subcontract greater than the simplified acquisition threshold for other than commercial items, the contractor is required to determine the following:

1. If commercial items or nondevelopmental items can meet the agency's requirements, could be modified to meet the agency's requirements or could meet the agency's requirements if such requirements were modified to a reasonable extent, and

2. The extent to which commercial or nondevelopmental items could be incorporated at the component level.

FAR Part 11. Describing Agency Needs

A. Policy (FAR 11.002)

Agencies shall specify needs using market research in a manner designed to promote full and open competition and only include restrictive provisions or conditions to the extent necessary to satisfy the needs of the agency or as authorized by law.

Acquisition officials should state requirements with respect to an acquisition of supplies or services in terms of

- Functions to be performed,

- Performance required, or

- Essential physical characteristics.

Acquisition officials should define requirements in terms that enable and encourage offerors to supply commercial items, or to the extent that commercial items suitable to meet the agency's needs are not available, nondevelopmental items, in response to the agency solicitations. Offerors of commercial items and nondevelopmental items should be provided an opportunity to compete in any acquisition to fill such requirements. Prime contractors and subcontractors at all tiers should be required to incorporate commercial items or nondevelopmental items as components of items supplied to the agency. Requirements (in appropriate cases) should be modified to ensure that they can be met by commercial items or, to the extent that commercial items suitable to meet the agency's needs are not available, nondevelopmental items.

In the process of defining government requirements for products and services, various statutes and executive orders require consideration of sustainable acquisition, including energy-efficient and water-efficient products and services that may utilize renewable energy technologies, recovered materials, bio-based products, and other environmentally preferable products and services, including EPEAT-registered electronic products.

B. Delivery or Performance Schedules (FAR 11.4)

Time of delivery/performance must be realistic and clearly stated within the solicitation. Unreasonable delivery or performance schedules are inconsistent with small business policy, may restrict competition, and may result in higher contract prices. Factors to be considered in establishing schedules are listed in FAR 11.402.

Contract delivery or performance may be expressed in terms of specific calendar dates; specific periods from the date of the contract or from the date of receipt by the contractor of the notice of award or acceptance by the government; or specific time for delivery after receipt by the contractor of each individual order issued under the contract.

C. Liquidated Damages (FAR 11.5)

This section contains policies and procedures for using liquidated damages clauses in solicitations and contracts for supplies, services, research and development, and construction. This subpart does not apply to liquidated damages for subcontracting plans (see 19.705-7) or liquidated damages related to the Contract Work Hours and Safety Standards Act (see Subpart 22.3).

The contracting officer must consider the potential impact on pricing, competition, and contract administration before using a liquidated damages clause. Liquidated damages clauses should be used only when (1) the time of delivery or timely performance is so important that the government may reasonably expect to suffer damage if the delivery or performance is delinquent, and (2) the extent or amount of such damage would be difficult or impossible to estimate accurately or prove.

D. Priorities and Allocations (FAR 11.6)

The Defense Priorities and Allocations System (DPAS) authorizes the use of priorities to require that contracts in support of the national defense be accepted and performed on a preferential or priority basis over all other contracts, and to allocate materials and facilities in such a manner as to promote the national defense.

There are two levels of priority, identified by the rating symbols "DO" and "DX." DO rated orders have equal priority with each other and take preference over unrated orders. DX rated orders have equal priority with each other and take preference over both DO rated and unrated orders.

E. Variation in Quantity (FAR 11.7)

The government may authorize the acceptance of a variation in the quantities delivered under a fixed-price supply contract. There should be no standard or usual variation percentage, and the variance amount should be based on the normal commercial practices of a particular industry. Generally the difference should not exceed 10 percent.

FAR Part 12. Acquisition of Commercial Items

This part contains the policies and procedures unique to contracting for commercial items and implements the federal government's preference for commercial items.

A. Acquisition of Commercial Items— General (FAR 12.1)

It is policy that the government acquire commercial or nondevelopmental items whenever they are available and to require prime contractors and subcontractors at all tiers to incorporate commercial and nondevelopmental products as components whenever possible.

Contracting officers shall use commercial item procedures for any acquisition of supplies or services that meet the definition of "commercial item" found at FAR 2.101. Other circumstances where contracting officers may also use commercial item procedures are listed in FAR 12.102.

FAR Part 12 does not apply to the acquisition of commercial items at or below the micro-purchase threshold, or those acquired using the Standard Form 44, using the imprest fund, using the governmentwide commercial purchase card, or directly from another federal agency.

In general, all provisions that apply to commercial items also apply to commercially available off-the-shelf items.

B. Special Requirements for the Acquisition of Commercial Items (FAR 12.2)

Public Law 103-355 establishes special requirements for the acquisition of commercial items intended to more closely resemble those customarily used in the commercial marketplace.

Contracting officers shall use the policies unique to the acquisition of commercial items prescribed in this part in conjunction with the policies and procedures in Parts 13, 14, or 15, as appropriate for the particular acquisition. For acquisitions of commercial items exceeding the simplified acquisition threshold but not exceeding $6.5 million ($12 million for acquisitions as described in 13.500(e)), including options, contracting activities shall employ the simplified procedures authorized by Subpart 13.5 to the maximum extent practicable.

The contracting officer shall use the Standard Form (SF) 1449, Solicitation/Contract/Order for Commercial Items, if the acquisition is expected to exceed the simplified acquisition threshold, a paper solicitation or contract is being issued, and streamlined solicitation procedures are not being used. The use of the SF 1449 is not mandatory, but encouraged for commercial acquisitions not exceeding the SAT.

Where technical information is required to effectively evaluate offers, agencies should review existing product literature in lieu of technical proposals whenever possible. Agencies should also allow offerors to propose more than one product that will meet government needs, and contracting officers shall evaluate each product as a separate offer.

Past performance should be an important element of every evaluation and contract award for commercial items.

Agencies shall use firm-fixed-price contracts or fixed-price contracts with economic price adjustment for the acquisition of commercial items except as provided in FAR 12.207(b).

Contracts for commercial items shall rely on a contractor's existing quality assurance systems as a substitute for government inspection and testing unless other customary market practices exist.

The contracting officer must establish price reasonableness in accordance with the appropriate *FAR* clauses, and should also be aware of customary commercial terms and conditions that may affect the pricing being provided to the government.

If it is standard market practice for some commercial items to include buyer contract financing, the contracting officer may offer government financing in accordance with FAR Part 32.

Unless it is mandated by agency specific statute, the government acquires only the technical data and the rights in that data that are provided to the general public with the commercial item. The contracting officer shall assume the data was developed exclusively at private expense. If the government requires technical data rights, the contracting officer must include specific contract clauses.

Commercial computer software and documentation shall be acquired under licenses customarily provided to the public to the extent that those licenses are consistent with federal law and satisfy the government needs. In general, the contractor will not be required to furnish any technical information that is not customarily provided to the public or to give the government rights to use, modify, reproduce, release, perform, display, or disclose the software except as mutually agreed. The government shall have only those rights specified in the license.

The contracting officer has the discretion to incorporate other commercial terms in any contract if they are deemed appropriate to finalizing an arrangement that is satisfactory to both parties and are not precluded by law or executive order.

Cost Accounting Standards (CAS) do not apply to contracts and subcontracts for the acquisition of commercial items unless the contract provides for an economic price adjustment based on actual costs incurred. (FAR 12.214)

C. Solicitation Provisions and Contract Clauses for the Acquisition of Commercial Items (FAR 12.3)

Notwithstanding prescriptions contained elsewhere in the *FAR*, contracting officers shall be required to use only those provisions and clauses prescribed in Part 12. The contracting officer may include other *FAR* provisions and clauses by addendum when their use is consistent with the limitations on tailoring of provisions and clauses found in FAR 12.302. (FAR 12.301)

Limitations on tailoring of contract terms are found at FAR 12.302. The contracting officer shall not tailor any clause or otherwise include any additional terms or conditions in a solicitation or contract for commercial items in a manner that is inconsistent with customary commercial practice for the item being acquired unless a waiver is approved in accordance with agency procedures. The request for waiver must describe the customary commercial practice found in the marketplace, support the need to include a term or condition that is inconsistent with that practice, and include a determination that use of the customary commercial practice is inconsistent with the needs of the government.

D. Unique Requirements Regarding Terms and Conditions for Commercial Items (FAR 12.4)

This part provides guidance on tailoring specific paragraphs in 52.212-4, "Contract Terms and Conditions—Commercial Items," when the paragraphs do not reflect the customary practice, as well as guidance on administration when the terms differ substantially from those contained elsewhere in the *FAR*.

Acceptance: The clause is based on the assumption that the government will rely on the contractor's assurances that the commercial item conforms to the contract requirements. This paragraph is generally appropriate for non-complex acquisitions. Other provisions may be more appropriate for complex items or special situations. The government always retains the right to reject or refuse acceptance of nonconforming products.

Termination: The clause permits the government to terminate a contract for either convenience or cause. The government's rights after a termination for cause shall include all the remedies available to any buyer in the marketplace. The government's preferred remedy will be to acquire similar items from another contractor and to charge the defaulted contractor with any excess reprocurement costs together with any incidental or consequential damages incurred because of the termination.

Warranties: The government's post-award rights contained in 52.212-4 are the implied warranty of merchantability, the implied warranty of fitness for particular purpose, and the remedies contained in the acceptance paragraph. The implied warranty of merchantability provides that an item is reasonably fit for the ordinary purposes for which such items are used. The items must be of at least average, fair, or medium-grade quality and must be comparable in quality to those that will pass without objection in the trade or market for items of the same description.

The implied warranty of fitness for a particular purpose provides that an item is fit for use for the particular purpose for which the government will use the items. The government can rely upon an implied warranty of fitness for particular purpose when (1) the seller knows the particular purpose for which the government intends to use the item; and (2) the government relied upon the contractor's skill and judgment that the item would be appropriate for that particular purpose.

In some markets, it may be customary commercial practice for contractors to exclude or limit the implied warranties contained in 52.212-4 in the provisions of an express warranty. In such cases, the contracting officer shall ensure that the express warranty provides for the repair or replacement of defective items discovered within a reasonable period of time after acceptance. Express warranties shall be included in the contract by addendum.

E. Applicability of Certain Laws to Executive Agency Contracts for the Acquisition of Commercial Items (FAR 12.5)

A list of laws not applicable to executive agency contracts is found in this section.

H. Streamlined Procedures for Evaluation and Solicitation for Commercial Items (FAR 12.6)

Streamlined procedures are intended to simplify the process of preparing and issuing solicitations, and evaluating offers for commercial items consistent with customary commercial practices. When a written solicitation will be issued, the contracting officer may combine the GPE synopsis and the solicitation into a single document.

Section

THREE

FAR Parts 13–14

A. Policy (FAR Part 13)

Simplified acquisition procedures are those methods prescribed in FAR Part 13 for making purchases of supplies and services, including construction, research and development, and commercial items, the aggregate of which does not exceed the simplified acquisition threshold. Simplified acquisition methods include purchase orders, blanket purchase agreements, governmentwide commercial purchase cards, imprest funds, and third-party drafts. The processes may also be used for commercial items acquisitions that do not exceed $6.5 million (or $12 million for acquisitions described in 13.500(e)).

Use of such procedures reduces administrative costs, improves opportunities for small business and small disadvantaged business concerns to obtain a fair proportion of government contracts, promotes efficiency and economy in contracting, and avoids unnecessary burdens for agencies and contractors.

These procedures should be used for all purchases of supplies or services not exceeding the simplified acquisition threshold (including purchases below the micro-purchase threshold), unless requirements can be met by using required sources of supply under FAR Part 8 (such as Federal Prison Industries), existing indefinite delivery/indefinite quantity contracts, or other established contracts.

Certain acquisitions may be set aside for small businesses. Generally, each acquisition of supplies or services that has an anticipated dollar value exceeding $3,000 and not exceeding $150,000 is reserved exclusively for small business concerns and shall be set aside. Some exceptions to this are detailed in FAR Part 19.

The contracting officer may set aside for HUBZone small business concerns or service-disabled veteran–owned small business concerns an acquisition of supplies or services that has an anticipated dollar value exceeding the micro-purchase threshold and not exceeding the simplified acquisition threshold. The contracting officer's decision not to set aside an acquisition for HUBZone small business or service-disabled veteran-owned small business concerns participation below the simplified acquisition threshold is not subject to review under FAR 19.4.

Each written solicitation under a set-aside shall contain the appropriate provisions prescribed by Part 19. If the solicitation is oral, however, information substantially identical to that in the provision shall be given to potential quoters.

The contracting officer shall not use simplified acquisition procedures to acquire supplies and services if the anticipated award will exceed the simplified acquisition threshold, or $6.5 million ($12 million for acquisitions as described in 13.500(e)), including options, for acquisitions of commercial items using Subpart 13.5.

Do not break down requirements aggregating more than the simplified acquisition threshold (or for commercial items, the threshold in Subpart 13.5) or the micro-purchase threshold into several purchases that are less than the applicable threshold merely to permit use of simplified acquisition procedures, or avoid any requirement that applies to purchases exceeding the micro-purchase threshold.

In addition to other considerations, contracting officers are to

- Promote competition to the maximum extent practicable,

- Establish reasonable deadlines for submission of responses to solicitations,

- Consider all quotations or offers that are received on time, and

- Use innovative approaches to the maximum extent practicable.

A quotation is not an offer, and consequently, cannot be accepted by the government to form a binding contract. A contract comes into being when the supplier accepts the order (i.e., through confirmation in writing) by furnishing the requested supplies, or by proceeding with the work to the point where substantial performance has occurred.

FAR Parts 13.005 and 13.006 list inapplicable laws and contract provisions for goods and services purchased using the simplified acquisition method.

B. Procedures (FAR 13.1)

The contracting officer must promote competition to the maximum extent practicable to obtain supplies and services from the source whose offer is the most advantageous to the government, considering the administrative cost of the purchase. Contracting officers should use the Central Contractor Registration database as the primary source of vendor information. Contracting officers need not solicit a new quotation for each purchase, but may instead use a standing price quotation as long as it is current and the government obtains the maximum benefit of any discounts before award.

The contracting officer must not solicit quotations based on personal preference, or restrict solicitation to suppliers of well-known and widely distributed makes or brands.

Clearly articulate the basis—price alone or price and other factors (e.g., past performance and quality) upon which award will be made. It is not, however, necessary to state the relative importance assigned to each evaluation factor.

Solicitation from one source is authorized if the contracting officer determines that the circumstances of the contract action deem only one source reasonably available (e.g., urgency, exclusive licensing agreement).

Options may be included in solicitations, provided the requirements of FAR 17.2 are met and the aggregate value of the acquisition and all options does not exceed the dollar threshold for use of simplified acquisition procedures.

The contracting officer has broad discretion in fashioning suitable evaluation procedures. Those described in FAR Parts 14 and 15 are not mandatory; however, at the contracting officer's discretion, one or more, but not necessarily all, of the evaluation procedures in FAR Parts 14 and 15 may be used.

If using price and other factors, ensure that quotations or offers can be evaluated in an efficient and minimally burdensome fashion. Formal evaluation plans and establishing a competitive range, conducting discussions, and scoring quotations or offers are not required. Rather, contracting officers are encouraged to comparatively evaluate offers and to evaluate other factors (e.g., past performance) based on information such as knowledge of and previous experience with the supply or service being acquired.

Prior to award, the contracting officer must determine that the proposed price is fair and reasonable. Whenever possible, base price reasonableness on competitive quotations or offers. However, when this is not possible, this determination may be based on market research; comparison of the proposed price with prices found reasonable on previous purchases; current price lists, catalogs, or advertisements; a comparison with similar items in a related industry; value analysis; personal knowledge of the item being purchased; comparison to an independent government estimate; or any other reasonable basis.

In making purchases, contracting officers should

- Include related items (such as small hardware items or spare parts for vehicles) in one solicitation and make award on an "all-or-none" or "multiple award" basis, provided suppliers are so advised when quotations or offers are requested;

- Incorporate provisions and clauses by reference in solicitations and in awards under requests for quotations, provided the requirements in 52.102 are satisfied;

- Make maximum effort to obtain trade and prompt payment discounts. (FAR 14.408-3) Prompt payment discounts shall not be considered in the evaluation of quotations; and

- Use bulk funding to the maximum extent practicable. Bulk funding is a system whereby the contracting officer receives authorization from a fiscal and accounting officer to obligate funds on purchase documents against a specified lump sum of funds reserved for the purpose for a specified period of time rather than obtaining individual obligational authority on each purchase document. Bulk funding is particularly appropriate if numerous purchases using the same type of funds are to be made during a given period.

C. Actions At or Below the Micro-Purchase Threshold (FAR 13.2)

The governmentwide commercial purchase card is the preferred method to purchase and to pay for micro-purchases.

Purchases at or below the micro-purchase threshold may be conducted using any of the methods described in FAR 13.3, provided the purchaser is authorized and trained, pursuant to agency procedures, to use those methods.

Micro-purchases may be awarded without soliciting competitive quotations if the contracting officer determines that the price is reasonable. Action to verify price reasonableness should be taken only when the contracting officer suspects or has information to indicate that the price may not be reasonable or when purchasing a supply or service for which no comparable pricing information is readily available.

Micro-purchase procedures may also be used for certain contingency operations or defense against or recovery from attacks. The acquisition may not exceed $15,000 for contracts awarded and performed in the United States, or $30,000 if awarded and performed outside of the United States.

D. Simplified Acquisition Methods (13.3)

Governmentwide Commercial Purchase Card (FAR 13.301)

The governmentwide commercial purchase card is authorized for use in making and/or paying for purchases of supplies, services, or construction and may be used by contracting officers and other designated individuals. The card may be used only for purchases that are otherwise authorized by law or regulation.

The governmentwide commercial purchase card may be used to make micro-purchases; place a task or delivery order (if authorized in the basic contract, basic ordering agreement, or blanket purchase agreement); or make payments, when the contractor agrees to accept payment by the card.

Purchase Orders (FAR 13.302)

A purchase order is an offer by the government to buy supplies or services, including construction and research and development, upon specified terms and conditions, using simplified acquisition procedures. Except as provided under the unpriced purchase order method, purchase orders are to be issued on a fixed-price basis. Electronic funds transfer (EFT) is required for most payments. When obtaining oral quotes, the contracting officer shall inform the quoter of the EFT clause that will be in any resulting purchase order.

Unpriced purchase orders are orders for supplies or services, the price of which is not established at the time of issuance of the order. An example of this would be repairs to equipment that require disassembly to determine the nature or extent of repairs. Restrictions for use are listed in FAR 13.302-2.

Written acceptance of purchase order modifications is not required unless determined by the contracting officer to be necessary to ensure the contractor's compliance with the purchase order or otherwise required by agency regulation.

If the contractor has accepted a purchase order, the contracting officer shall proceed with the termination procedure appropriate for the item covered by the order, which is either the commercial item or noncommercial item procedure. If the purchase order has not been accepted in writing, the contracting officer shall notify the contractor in writing that the order has been cancelled and request written acceptance from the contractor. If that acceptance is received, the order is considered cancelled and no further action is required. If the contractor attempts to recover costs from starting performance it shall be handled as either a commercial item or noncommercial item termination.

Blanket Purchase Agreements (FAR 13.303)

A blanket purchase agreement (BPA) is a simplified method of filling anticipated repetitive needs for supplies or services by establishing "charge accounts" with qualified sources of supply.

BPAs are appropriate (1) when requirements exist for a wide variety of items within a broad class of goods, but the exact items, quantities, and delivery requirements are not known in advance; (2) when there is a need to provide commercial sources of supply for one or more offices in a given area that do not have or need authority to purchase otherwise; (3) when the writing of numerous purchase orders can be avoided through the use of this procedure; or (4) when there is no existing requirements contract for the same supply or service that the contracting activity is required to use.

After determining that a BPA would be advantageous, contracting officers should establish the parameters to limit purchases to individual items or commodity groups or classes, or permit the supplier to furnish unlimited supplies or services. Contracting officers should consider suppliers whose past performance has shown them to be dependable, who offer quality supplies or services at consistently lower prices, and who have provided numerous purchases at or below the simplified acquisition threshold.

BPAs may be established with more than one supplier for supplies or services of the same type to provide maximum practicable competition; a single firm from which numerous individual purchases at or below the simplified acquisition threshold will likely be made in a given period; or Federal Supply Schedule contractors, if not inconsistent with the terms of the applicable schedule contract.

BPAs include a description of the agreement, the extent of obligation, pricing, purchase limitations, notice of individuals authorized to place orders, delivery tickets, and invoices. They are considered complete when the purchases under them equal their total dollar limitation, if any, or when their stated time period expires.

Imprest Funds and Third-Party Drafts (FAR 13.305)

An *imprest fund* is a cash fund of a fixed amount established by an advance of funds, without charge to an appropriation, from an agency finance or disbursing officer to a duly appointed cashier, for disbursement as needed from time to time in making payment in cash for relatively small purchases.

A *third-party draft* means an agency bank draft, similar to a check that is used to acquire and to pay for supplies and services.

Either imprest funds or third-party drafts may be used for purchases when

- The imprest fund transaction does not exceed $500;

- The third-party draft transaction does not exceed $2,500;

- Use of imprest funds or third party drafts is considered advantageous to the government; and

- The use of imprest funds or third-party drafts for the transaction otherwise complies with any additional conditions established by agencies and with the policies and regulations.

Purchases made using imprest funds or third-party drafts shall be based upon an authorized purchase requisition, contracting officer verification statement, or another agency approved method of ensuring that adequate funds are available for the purchase. Normally, purchases should be placed orally and without soliciting competition if prices are considered reasonable. Clauses are not required for purchases using imprest funds or third-party drafts.

The SF 44 Purchase Order-Invoice-Voucher

The SF 44 Purchase Order-Invoice-Voucher is a multipurpose pocket-sized purchase order form designed primarily for on-the-spot, over-the-counter purchases of supplies and nonpersonal services while away from the purchasing office or at isolated activities. It may be used when (1) the amount of the purchase is at or below the micro-purchase threshold, (2) the supplies or services are immediately available, (3) one delivery and one payment will be made, and (4) its use is determined to be more economical and efficient than use of other simplified acquisition procedures. The form may also be used as a receiving report, invoice, or public voucher as needed.

E. Fast Payment Procedure (FAR 13.4)

The fast payment procedure allows payment under limited conditions to a contractor prior to the government's verification that supplies have been received and accepted. They are generally used when an individual order does not exceed $30,000 and delivery must occur at a geographically separated location that would make it impractical to make timely payment based on evidence of government acceptance.

It provides for payment based on the contractor's submission of an invoice, which constitutes the contractor's representation that supplies have been delivered to a post office, common carrier, or point of first receipt by the government; and that the contractor agrees to replace, repair, or correct supplies not received at destination, damaged in transit, or not conforming to the purchase agreement. Title to the supplies passes to the government upon delivery to a post office or common carrier for mailing or shipment to destination (or upon receipt by the government, if the shipment is by means other than Postal Service or common carrier).

The contracting officer shall be primarily responsible for determining the amounts of debts resulting from failure of contractors to properly replace, repair, or correct supplies that have been lost, damaged, or not conforming to purchase requirements.

FAR Part 14. Sealed Bidding

A. Use of Sealed Bidding (FAR 14.1)

Sealed bidding is a method of contracting that employs competitive bids, public opening of bids, and awards. Specific steps include preparing an invitation for bids, publicizing the invitation, submission of bids, evaluating the bids, and awarding the contract.

Award is made to the responsible bidder whose bid is responsive to the terms of the invitation for bids (IFB) and is most advantageous to the government, considering only price and price-related factors included in the invitation.

Sealed bidding can only be used with firm-fixed-price and fixed-price with economic price adjustment contracts.

B. Solicitation of Bids (FAR 14.2)

To the extent practicable, IFBs are to conform to the uniform contract format; however, for acquisitions of supplies and services, the simplified contract format may be used instead.

To avoid unduly restricting competition or paying higher-than-necessary prices, reasonable bidding times are to be established based upon degree of urgency, complexity of requirement, anticipated extent of subcontracting, whether use was made of presolicitation notices, geographic distribution of bidders, and normal transmittal time for both invitations and bids. However, for those actions over the simplified acquisition thresholds, at least 30 calendar days' bidding time must be provided when synopsis is required.

A *bid sample* is a sample to be furnished by a bidder to show the characteristics of a product offered in a bid. Bidders shall not be required to furnish bid samples unless there are characteristics of the product that cannot be described adequately in the specification or purchase description. Bid samples will be used only to determine the responsiveness of the bid and will not be used to determine a bidder's ability to produce the required items. Bid samples may be examined for any required characteristic, whether or not such characteristic is adequately described in the specification. Bids will be rejected as nonresponsive if the sample fails to conform to each of the characteristics listed in the invitation. Bid samples are appropriate for products that must be suitable from the standpoint of balance, facility of use, general "feel," color, pattern, or other characteristics that cannot be described adequately in the specification. However, when more than a minor portion of the characteristics of the product cannot be adequately described in the specification, products should be acquired by two-step sealed bidding or negotiation, as appropriate.

Descriptive literature means information, such as cuts, illustrations, drawings, and brochures, which shows the characteristics or construction of a product or explains its operation. It is furnished by bidders as a part of their bids to describe the products offered. The term includes only information required to determine acceptability of the product. It excludes other information such as that furnished in connection with the qualifications of a bidder or for use in operating or maintaining equipment. Bidders shall not be required to furnish descriptive literature unless the contracting office needs it to determine before award whether the products offered meet the specification and to establish exactly what the bidder proposes to furnish. The reasons why product acceptability cannot be determined without the submission of descriptive literature shall be set forth in the contract file, except when such submission is required by formal specifications (federal, military, or other) applicable to the acquisition. The contracting officer has the authority to waive the requirement for descriptive literature.

When a bid is accompanied by descriptive literature, and the bidder imposes a restriction that prevents the public disclosure of such literature, the restriction may render the bid nonresponsive. The restriction renders the bid nonresponsive if it prohibits the disclosure of sufficient information to permit competing bidders to know the essential nature and type of the products offered or those elements of the bid that relate to quantity, price, and delivery terms. The provisions of this paragraph do not apply to unsolicited descriptive literature submitted by a bidder if such literature does not qualify the bid.

Solicitation mailing lists must be maintained by contracting activities to ensure access to adequate sources of supplies/services, except when the requirements can be satisfied through the use of simplified acquisition procedures, the requirements are non-recurring or electronic commerce methods are used.

A concern may be removed from the mailing list for a specific item if they fail to respond to the presolicitation notice, submit a bid, or otherwise respond to the IFB.

Contracting officers may authorize facsimile bids. If facsimile bids are authorized, contracting officers may, after the date set for bid opening, request the apparently successful offeror to provide the complete, original signed bid. Contracting officers may also authorize use of electronic commerce for submission of bids. If electronic bids are authorized, the solicitation shall specify the electronic commerce method(s) that bidders may use.

A pre-bid conference may be used, generally in a complex acquisition, as a means of briefing prospective bidders and explaining complicated specifications and requirements. It shall never be used as a substitute for amending a defective or ambiguous invitation.

IFBs should not be canceled unless cancellation is clearly in the public interest; (e.g., where there is no longer a requirement for the supplies or services or where amendments to the invitation would be of such magnitude that a new invitation is desirable).

Discussions with prospective bidders regarding a solicitation shall be conducted and technical or other information shall be transmitted only by the contracting officer or superiors having contractual authority or by others specifically authorized. Such personnel shall not furnish any information to a prospective bidder that alone or together with other information may afford an advantage over others. However, general information that would not be prejudicial to other prospective bidders may be furnished upon request; (e.g., explanation of a particular contract clause or a particular condition of the schedule in the invitation for bids, and more specific information or clarifications may be furnished by amending the solicitation).

C. Submission of Bids (FAR 14.3)

A bid must comply with all material aspects of the invitation to be considered for award. It must be received in the office designated in the IFB no later than the exact time set for bid opening. It may be withdrawn or modified by written or telegraphic notice no later than the exact time set for bid opening.

Bidders are responsible for submitting bids so as to reach the government office designated in the IFB by the time specified in the IFB. If no time is specified, the time for receipt is 4:30 p.m. local time, for the designated government office on the date that bids are due. Acceptable evidence to establish the time of receipt at the government installation includes the time/date stamp of such installation on the bid wrapper, other documentary evidence of receipt maintained by the installation, or oral testimony or statements of government personnel.

Late bids that are not considered for award are to be held unopened, unless opened for identification, until after award and then retained with other unsuccessful bids.

D. Opening of Bids and Award of Contract (FAR 14.4)

All bids received before the time set for the opening of bids must be kept secure, generally locked in a bid box, safe, or in a secured, restricted-access electronic bid box. At bid opening, the bid opening officer personally and publicly opens all bids received, reads the bids aloud to those present, and ensures that bids are recorded.

Bid openings may be postponed if the contracting officer believes that bids have been delayed in the mail for causes beyond the control of potential bidders or if emergency or unanticipated events interrupt normal governmental processes rendering bid opening impractical.

Cancellation of IFBs after opening may be done only after the agency head determines it to be appropriate in accordance with FAR 14.404-1.

Preservation of the integrity of the competitive bid system dictates that after bids have been opened, award must be made to that responsible bidder who submitted the lowest responsive bid, unless there is a compelling reason to reject all bids and cancel the invitation.

Individual bids may be rejected for any of the follow reasons:

- Any bid that fails to conform to the essential requirements of the invitation for bids shall be rejected.

- Any bid that does not conform to the applicable specifications shall be rejected unless the invitation authorized the submission of alternate bids and the supplies offered as alternates meet the requirements specified in the invitation.

- Any bid that fails to conform to the delivery schedule or permissible alternates stated in the invitation shall be rejected.

- A bid shall be rejected when the bidder imposes conditions that would modify requirements of the invitation or limit the bidder's liability to the government, since to allow the bidder to impose such conditions would be prejudicial to other bidders.

For example, bids shall be rejected in which the bidder

- Protects against future changes in conditions, such as increased costs, if total possible costs to the government cannot be determined;

- Fails to state a price and indicates that price shall be "price in effect at time of delivery;"

- States a price but qualifies it as being subject to "price in effect at time of delivery;"

- When not authorized by the invitation, conditions or qualifies a bid by stipulating that it is to be considered only if, before date of award, the bidder receives (or does not receive) award under a separate solicitation;

- Requires that the government is to determine that the bidder's product meets applicable government specifications; or

- Limits rights of the government under any contract clause.

- A low bidder may be requested to delete objectionable conditions from a bid provided the conditions do not go to the substance, as distinguished from the form, of the bid, or work an injustice on other bidders. A condition goes to the substance of a bid where it affects price, quantity, quality, or delivery of the items offered.

Any bid may be rejected if the contracting officer determines in writing that it is unreasonable as to price. Unreasonableness of price includes not only the total price of the bid, but the prices for individual line items as well.

Any bid may be rejected if the prices for any line items or sub-line items are materially unbalanced.

Bids received from any person or concern that is suspended, debarred, proposed for debarment, or declared ineligible as of the bid opening date shall be rejected unless a compelling reason determination is made (see Subpart 9.4). Low bids received from concerns determined to be not responsible pursuant to Subpart 9.1 shall be rejected (but if a bidder is a small business concern, see 19.6 with respect to certificates of competency).

Generally, when a bid guarantee is required and a bidder fails to furnish the guarantee in accordance with the requirements of the invitation for bids, the bid shall be rejected.

The originals of all rejected bids, and any written findings with respect to such rejections, shall be preserved with the papers relating to the acquisition.

After submitting a bid, if all of a bidder's assets or that part related to the bid are transferred during the period between the bid opening and the award, the transferee may not be able to take over the bid. Accordingly, the contracting officer shall reject the bid unless the transfer is affected by merger, operation of law, or other means not barred by 41 U.S.C. 15 or 31 U.S.C. 3727.

A minor informality or irregularity is one that is merely a matter of form and not of substance. In cases of apparent mistakes and in cases where the contracting officer has reason to believe that a mistake may have been made, he or she must request from the bidder a verification of the bid, calling attention to the suspected mistake. Clerical mistakes, apparent on its face, may be corrected before award.

The authority to permit correction of bids is limited to bids that, as submitted, are responsive to the IFB and may not be used to permit correction of bids to make them responsive.

Mistakes after award are processed in accordance with FAR 14.407-4.

Contracts are awarded in the following order of priority in the case of equal low bids: small business concerns that are also labor surplus area concerns, other small business concerns, and then, other business concerns.

E. Two-Step Sealed Bidding (FAR 14.5)

Two-step bidding is a combination of competitive procedures designed to obtain the benefits of sealed bidding when adequate specifications are not available. Step one consists of request for submission, evaluation, and discussion of technical proposals. Step two consists of submission of sealed bids by those who submitted acceptable technical proposals in step one.

Unless other factors require the use of sealed bidding, two-step sealed bidding may be used in preference to negotiation when all of the following conditions are present:

1. Available specifications or purchase descriptions are not definite or complete or may be too restrictive without technical evaluation, and any necessary discussion, of the technical aspects of the requirement to ensure mutual understanding between each source and the government;

2. Definite criteria exist for evaluating technical proposals;

3. More than one technically qualified source is expected to be available;

4. Sufficient time will be available for use of the two-step method; and

5. A firm-fixed-price contract or a fixed-price contract with economic price adjustment will be used.

Section

FOUR

FAR Part 15

This part prescribes policies and procedures governing competitive and noncompetitive negotiated acquisitions. A contract awarded using other than sealed bidding procedures is a negotiated contract.

A. Source Selection Processes and Techniques (FAR 15.1)

Best value is best seen as a continuum wherein best value can be obtained through the use of any one or a combination of source selection approaches. As an example, in acquisitions where the requirement is clearly definable and the risk of unsuccessful contract performance is minimal, cost or price may play a dominant role in source selection. The less definitive the requirement, the more development work required; or the greater the performance risk, the more technical or past performance considerations may play a dominant role in source selection.

A tradeoff process is appropriate when it may be in the best interest of the government to consider award to other than the lowest priced offeror or other than the highest technically rated offeror. This process permits tradeoffs among cost or price and noncost factors and allows the government to accept other than the lowest priced proposal or other than the highest technically rated offeror.

Oral presentations by offerors as requested by the government may substitute for, or augment, written information. They may occur at any time in the acquisition process, and are subject to the same restrictions as written information, regarding timing and content.

When an oral presentation includes information that the parties intend to include in the contract as material terms and conditions, the information shall be put in writing. Incorporation by reference of oral statement is not permitted.

B. Solicitation and Receipt of Proposals and Information (FAR 15.2)

To improve the understanding of government requirements and industry capabilities—thereby allowing potential offerors to judge whether or how they can satisfy the government's requirements, enhancing the government's ability to obtain quality supplies and services, at reasonable prices, and increasing efficiency in proposal preparation, proposal evaluation, negotiation, and contract award—exchanges of information among all interested parties, from the earliest identification of a requirement through receipt of proposals, are encouraged.

Techniques to promote early exchanges of information include industry or small business conferences, market research, one-on-one meetings with potential offerors, presolicitation notices, draft requests for proposals (RFPs), requests for information (RFIs), presolicitation or preproposal conferences, and site visits.

RFIs may be used when the government does not presently intend to award a contract, but wants to obtain price, delivery, other market information, or capabilities for planning purposes. Responses to these notices are not offers and cannot be accepted by the government to form a binding contract. There is no required format for RFIs.

RFPs are used to communicate government requirements to prospective contractors and to solicit proposals. RFPs for competitive acquisitions must describe the government's requirement, anticipated terms and conditions that will apply to the contract, information required to be in the offeror's proposal, and factors and significant subfactors that will be used to evaluate the proposal and their relative importance. RFPs for noncompetitive acquisitions should be tailored to remove unnecessary information and requirements.

Unless specifically excluded elsewhere in the *FAR*, solicitations and resulting contracts are to be formatted in accordance with the uniform contract format outlined in Table 15-1. Solicitations using the uniform contract format shall include Part I (The Schedule, which includes sections A through H); Part II (Contract Clauses, which is section I), Part III (List of Documents, Exhibits, and Other Attachments, which is section J); and Part IV (Representations and Instructions, which is sections K through M). Upon award, contracting officers shall not physically include Part IV in the resulting contract, but shall retain it in the contract file. Section K shall be incorporated by reference in the contract.

The solicitation is to be amended when (either before or after receipt of proposals) the government changes its requirements or terms and conditions.

Proposals, and modifications thereto, that are received in the designated government office after the exact time specified are "late" and shall be considered only if they are received before award is made and the circumstances meet the specific requirements of FAR 52.215-1(c)(3)(i).

Proposals may be withdrawn by written notice at any time before award. Written proposals are withdrawn upon receipt by the contracting officer of a written notice of withdrawal. Oral proposals in response to oral solicitations may be withdrawn orally before award and the contracting officer must document the contract file when oral withdrawals are made.

Acceptable evidence to establish the time of receipt at the government installation includes the time/date stamp of that installation on the proposal wrapper, other documentary evidence of receipt maintained by the installation, or oral testimony or statements of government personnel.

C. Source Selection (FAR 15.3)

The objective of source selection is to select the proposal that represents the best value.

The award decision is based on evaluation factors and significant subfactors that are tailored to the acquisition.

Evaluation factors and significant subfactors must represent the key areas of importance and emphasis to be considered in the source selection decision, and support meaningful comparison and discrimination between and among competing proposals.

The evaluation factors and significant subfactors that apply to an acquisition and their relative importance are within the broad discretion of agency acquisition officials, subject to the following requirements:

1. Price or cost to the government shall be evaluated in every source selection.

2. The quality of the product or service shall be addressed in every source selection through consideration of one or more noncost evaluation factors such as past performance, compliance with solicitation requirements, technical excellence, management capability, personnel qualifications, and prior experience; and

3. Past performance shall be evaluated in all source selections for negotiated competitive acquisitions expected to exceed the simplified acquisition threshold.

4. The extent of participation of small disadvantaged business concerns in performance of the contract shall be evaluated in unrestricted acquisitions expected to exceed $650,000 ($1.5 million for construction).

5. For solicitations involving bundling that offer a significant opportunity for subcontracting, the contracting officer must include proposed small business subcontracting participation in the subcontracting plan as an evaluation factor.

Competitive proposals are evaluated and assessed using the factors and subfactors specified in the solicitation. Proposal evaluation may be conducted using any rating method or combination of methods, including color or adjectival ratings, numerical weights, and ordinal rankings.

Normally, competition establishes price reasonableness. However, in limited situations, a cost analysis may be necessary to establish reasonableness of an otherwise successful offeror's price.

In evaluating past performance, the currency and relevance of the information, source of the information, context of the data, and general trends in a contractor's performance should be considered.

Clarifications are limited exchanges between the government and offerors that may occur when award without discussions is contemplated. An example would be providing offerors the opportunity to resolve minor or clerical errors or to clarify certain aspects of their proposal (i.e., the relevance of an offeror's past performance information).

If discussions are contemplated, the contracting officer must establish a competitive range comprised of the most highly rated proposals. Communications, then, are exchanges between the government and offerors after receipt of proposals, leading to establishment of the competitive range.

Negotiations are exchanges, in either a competitive or sole source environment, between the government and offerors that are undertaken with the intent of allowing the offeror to revise its proposal. When negotiations are conducted in a competitive acquisition, they take place after establishment of the competitive range and are called discussions.

Discussions are tailored to each offeror's proposal and must be conducted by the contracting officer with each offeror within the competitive range. The primary objective of discussions is to maximize the government's ability to obtain best value based on the requirement and the evaluation factors set forth in the solicitation. At a minimum, the contracting officer must indicate to or discuss with each offeror still being considered for award, deficiencies, significant weaknesses, and adverse past performance information to which the offeror has not yet had an opportunity to respond. The contracting officer also is encouraged to discuss other aspects of the offeror's proposal that could, in the opinion of the contracting officer, be altered or explained to enhance materially the proposal's potential for award. However, the contracting officer is not required to discuss every area where the proposal could be improved. The scope and extent of discussions are a matter of contracting officer judgment.

If, after discussions have begun, an offeror originally in the competitive range is no longer considered to be among the most highly rated offerors being considered for award, that offeror may be eliminated from the competitive range. Any offeror excluded or eliminated from the competitive range may request a debriefing.

Government personnel involved in the acquisition are not to engage in conduct that favors one offeror over another, reveals an offeror's technical solution or any information that would compromise an offeror's intellectual property to another offeror, reveals an offeror's price without that offeror's permission, reveal the names of individuals providing reference information about an offeror's past performance, or knowingly furnish source selection information.

If an offeror's proposal is eliminated or otherwise removed from the competitive range, no further revisions to that offeror's proposal shall be accepted or considered. The contract-

ing officer may request or allow proposal revisions to clarify and document understandings reached during negotiations. At the conclusion of discussions, each offeror still in the competitive range shall be given an opportunity to submit a final proposal revision. The contracting officer is required to establish a common cut-off date only for receipt of final proposal revisions. Requests for final proposal revisions shall advise offerors that the final proposal revisions shall be in writing and that the government intends to make award without obtaining further revisions.

The source selection authority's (SSA's) decision must be made independently, based on a comparative assessment of proposals against all source selection criteria in the solicitation.

D. Contract Pricing (FAR 15.4)

Cost or pricing data means all information that, as of the date of price agreement or, if applicable, an earlier date agreed upon between the parties that are as close as practicable to the date of agreement on price, is factual, not judgmental, and is verifiable. Cost or pricing data are data requiring certification.

Cost realism means that the costs in an offeror's proposal are realistic for the work to be performed; reflect a clear understanding of the requirements, and are consistent with the various elements of the offeror's technical proposal.

Information other than cost or pricing data means pricing data, cost data, and judgmental information that is not required to be certified and is necessary to determine price reasonableness or cost realism.

Price means cost plus any fee or profit applicable to the contract type.

Supplies and services are to be purchased from responsible sources at fair and reasonable prices. However, in establishing the reasonableness of price, contracting officers must not obtain more information than is necessary. When cost or pricing data are not required, they are to rely on the following, in order of preference, in determining the type of information required: no additional information, particularly if the price is based on adequate price competition; information other than cost or pricing data; and finally, cost or pricing data.

Cost or pricing data shall not be obtained for acquisitions at or below the simplified acquisition threshold.

Exceptions to cost or pricing data requirements: The contracting officer shall not require submission of cost or pricing data to support any action (contracts, subcontracts, or modifications), but may require information other than cost or pricing data to support a determination of price reasonableness or cost realism.

Cost analysis (the review and evaluation of the separate cost elements and profit in an offeror's or contractor's proposal and the application of judgment to determine how well the proposed costs represent what the cost of the contract should be, assuming reasonable economy and efficiency) is used to evaluate the reasonableness of individual cost elements when cost or pricing data are required. Price analysis should also be used to verify that the overall price offered is fair and reasonable. (Unless waived, the threshold for obtaining certified cost or pricing data is $700,000.)

Price analysis (the process of examining and evaluating a proposed price without evaluating its separate cost elements and proposed profit) is used when cost or pricing data are not required. However, cost analysis may also be used to evaluate information other than cost or pricing data to determine cost reasonableness or cost realism. The preferred techniques for price analysis are comparison of prices received in response to the solicitation and comparison with previously proposed prices with current proposed prices for the same or similar items, use of parametric estimating methods, comparison with competitive published price lists, and comparison of proposed prices with independent government cost estimates.

Field pricing assistance should be requested when the information available at the buying activity is inadequate to determine a fair and reasonable price. The contracting officer must tailor requests to reflect the minimum essential supplementary information needed to conduct a technical or cost or pricing analysis. Results may be reported directly to the contracting officer orally, in writing, or by any other method acceptable to him or her.

At a minimum, the contracting officer must use price analysis to determine whether the price is fair and reasonable when acquiring commercial items. The fact that a price is included in a catalog does not, in and of itself, make the price fair and reasonable. If the contracting officer cannot determine whether the offered price of a commercial item is fair and reasonable, even after obtaining additional information from sources other than the offeror, then the contracting officer must require the offeror to submit information other than cost or pricing data to support further analysis.

Price or fee may not exceed the following statutory limitations:

- For experimental, developmental, or research work performed under a cost-plus-fixed-fee contract, the fee shall not exceed 15 percent of the contract's estimated cost, excluding fee.

- For architect/engineer services for public works or utilities, the contract price or the estimated cost and fee for production and delivery of designs, plans, drawings, and specifications shall not exceed six percent of the estimated cost of construction of the public work or utility, excluding fees.

- For other cost-plus-fixed-fee contracts, the fee shall not exceed 10 percent of the contract's estimated cost, excluding fee.

If a change or modification calls for essentially the same type and mix of work as the basic contract and is of relatively small dollar value compared to the total contract value, the basic contract's profit or fee rate may be used as the pre-negotiation objective for that change or modification.

Contract type, cost, and profit or fee should be balanced to achieve an agreement that is fair and reasonable to both the government and the contractor.

The principal elements of the negotiated agreement are documented in a Price Negotiation Memorandum (PNM). Contents thereof are delineated in FAR 15.406-3.

The prime contractor is responsible for managing contract performance, including planning, placing, and administering subcontracts as necessary to ensure the lowest overall cost and technical risk to the government. When make-or-buy programs are required, the government may reserve the right to review and agree on the contractor's make-or-buy program when necessary to ensure negotiation of reasonable contract prices, satisfactory performance, or implementation of socioeconomic policies.

The contracting officer is responsible for the determination of a fair and reasonable price for the prime contract, including subcontracting costs. The contracting officer should consider whether a contractor or subcontractor has an approved purchasing system, has performed cost or price analysis of proposed subcontractor prices, or has negotiated the subcontract prices before negotiation of the prime contract, in determining the reasonableness of the prime contract price. This does not relieve the contracting officer from the responsibility to analyze the contractor's

submission, including the subcontractor's cost or pricing data.

The prime contractor or subcontractor shall conduct appropriate cost or price analyses to establish the reasonableness of proposed subcontract prices and, if required, submit subcontractor certified cost or pricing data to the government as part of its own certified cost or pricing data.

Any contractor or subcontractor that is required to submit certified cost or pricing data also shall obtain and analyze certified cost or pricing data before awarding any subcontract, purchase order, or modification expected to exceed the certified cost or pricing data threshold, unless an exception in 15.403-1(b) applies to that action.

The contractor shall submit certified cost or pricing data to the government for subcontracts that are the lower of either

- $12.5 million or more; or

- Both more than the pertinent certified cost or pricing data threshold and more than 10 percent of the prime contractor's proposed price, unless the contracting officer believes such submission is unnecessary.

The contracting officer may require the contractor or subcontractor to submit to the government subcontractor certified cost or pricing data below these thresholds and data other than certified cost or pricing data that the contracting officer considers necessary for adequately pricing the prime contract. If there is more than one prospective subcontractor for any given work, the contractor need only submit to the government certified cost or pricing data for the prospective subcontractor most likely to receive the award. If, before reaching agreement on price, the contracting officer learns that the certified cost or pricing data is inaccurate, incomplete, or noncurrent, the contractor may correct the deficiency for consideration. If, after award, certified cost or pricing data are found to be inaccurate, incomplete, or noncurrent, the government is entitled to a price adjustment, including profit or fee.

E. Pre-award, Award, and Post-award Notifications, Protests, and Mistakes (FAR 15.5)

Notifications to offerors eliminated from the competition shall be given promptly and shall include information that further proposal revisions will not be accepted. In the case of a small business program, notification shall also indicate if a set-aside was used, if a disadvantaged business received a benefit and is the apparent successful offeror, or when using the HUBZone, service-disabled–veteran or woman-owned small business programs.

Post-award notice must be provided to unsuccessful offerors within three days of contract award. The notice shall list the following:

1. The number of offerors solicited;

2. The number of proposals received;

3. The name and address of each offeror receiving an award;

4. The items, quantities, and any stated unit prices of each award, or if impractical, the total contract price. However, the items, quantities, and any stated unit prices of each award shall be made publicly available upon request; and

5. In general terms, the reason(s) the offeror's proposal was not accepted, unless the price information readily reveals the reason.

In no event shall an offeror's cost breakdown, profit, overhead rates, trade secrets, manufacturing processes and techniques, or other confidential business information be disclosed to any other offeror.

The contracting officer shall award a contract to the successful offeror by furnishing the executed contract or other notice of the award to that offeror.

Debriefings may be done orally, in writing, or by any other method acceptable to the contracting officer.

Pre-award Briefings:

1. An offeror may request a pre-award debriefing by submitting a written request for debriefing to the contracting officer within three days after receipt of a notice of exclusion from the competition.

2. Debriefings must include the agency's evaluation of significant elements in the offeror's proposal; a summary of the rationale for eliminating the offeror from the competition; and reasonable responses to relevant questions about whether source selection procedures contained in the solicitation, applicable regulations, and other applicable authorities were followed in the process of eliminating the offeror from the competition.

3. Debriefings shall not disclose the number of offerors; the identity of other offerors; the content of other offerors' proposals; the ranking of other offerors; the evaluation of other offerors; point-by-point comparisons of this offeror's proposal with those of other offerors; trade secrets; privileged or confidential manufacturing processes and techniques; commercial or financial information that is privileged or confidential, including cost breakdowns, profit, indirect cost rates, and similar information; and the names of individuals providing reference information about an offeror's past performance.

Post-award Briefings:

1. An offeror may request a post-award debriefing by submitting a written request

for debriefing to the contracting officer within three days after receipt of a notice of contract award. To the maximum extent practicable, the debriefing should occur within five days after receipt of the written request.

2. Debriefing must include the government's evaluation of the significant weaknesses or deficiencies in the offeror's proposal, if applicable; the overall evaluated cost or price and technical rating, if applicable, of the successful offeror and this offeror, and past performance information on this offeror; the overall ranking of all offerors, when any ranking was developed by the agency during the source selection; a summary of the rationale for award; for commercial items, the make and model of the item to be delivered by the successful offeror; and reasonable responses to relevant questions about whether source selection procedures contained in the solicitation, applicable regulations, and other applicable authorities were followed.

3. Debriefings shall not include point-by-point comparisons of this offeror's proposal with those of other offerors; trade secrets; privileged or confidential manufacturing processes and techniques; commercial or financial information that is privileged or confidential, including cost breakdowns, profit, indirect cost rates, and similar information; and the names of individuals providing reference information about an offeror's past performance.

F. Unsolicited Proposals (FAR 15.6)

An *unsolicited proposal* is a written proposal for a new or innovative idea that is submitted to an agency on the initiative of the offeror for the purpose of obtaining a contract with the government, and that is not in response to a request for proposals, broad agency announcement, small business innovation research topic, small business technology transfer research topic, program research and development announcement, or any other government-initiated solicitation or program.

Submission of new and innovative ideas in response to some type of government-initiated solicitation or program is preferred. Only when new or innovative ideas fall outside topic areas publicized under those programs or techniques can they be submitted as unsolicited proposals.

Agencies shall establish procedures for controlling the receipt, evaluation, and timely disposition of unsolicited proposals consistent with the requirements of this subpart. The procedures shall include controls on the reproduction and disposition of proposal material, particularly data identified by the offeror as subject to duplication, use, or disclosure restrictions.

A favorable comprehensive evaluation of an unsolicited proposal does not justify awarding a contract without providing for full and open competition. The agency point of contact shall return an unsolicited proposal to the offeror, citing reasons, when its substance

- Is available to the government without restriction from another source;

- Closely resembles a pending competitive acquisition requirement;

- Does not relate to the activity's mission; or

- Does not demonstrate an innovative and unique method, approach, or concept, or is otherwise not deemed a meritorious proposal.

The contracting officer may commence negotiations on a sole source basis only when

- An unsolicited proposal has received a favorable comprehensive evaluation;

- A justification and approval has been obtained for research proposals;

- The agency technical office sponsoring the contract furnishes the necessary funds; and

- The Contracting Officer has complied with the synopsis requirements.

Government personnel shall not use any data, concept, idea, or other part of an unsolicited proposal as the basis, or part of the basis, for a solicitation or in negotiations with any other firm unless the offeror is notified of and agrees to the intended use. However, this prohibition does not preclude using any data, concept, or idea in the proposal that also is available from another source without restriction.

Section

FIVE

FAR Parts 19, 22–25, 27–39

A. Size Standards (FAR 19.1)

FAR 19.101 gives an explanation of terms. In particular, it focuses on a wide variety of control issues that deal with whether to count "affiliates" for size determination purposes.

The SBA establishes small business size standards on an industry-by-industry basis. (See 13 CFR 121.) Small business size standards are applied by:

- Classifying the product or service being acquired in the industry whose definition, as found in the *North American Industry Classification System (NAICS) Manual* (available at **www.census.gov/epcd/www/naics. html**), best describes the principal nature of the product or service being acquired;

- Identifying the size standard SBA established for that industry; and

- Specifying the size standard in the solicitation so that offerors can appropriately represent themselves as small or large.

B. Policies (FAR 19.2)

The Small Business Act requires each agency to establish an Office of Small and Disadvantaged Business Utilization. The Department of Defense has renamed this the Office of Small Business Programs.

The contracting officer must, to the extent practicable, provide maximum participation opportunity to small business, veteran-owned small business, service-disabled veteran–owned small business, HUBZone small business, small disadvantaged business, economically disadvantaged woman-owned small business, and woman-owned small business concerns in acquisitions by taking the following actions:

65

1. Plan acquisitions such that, if practicable, more than one small business concern may perform the work;

2. Before issuing solicitations, make every reasonable effort to find additional small business concerns, unless lists are already excessively long and only some of the concerns on the list will be solicited. This effort should include contacting the agency SBA procurement center representative, or if there is none, the SBA;

3. Publicize solicitations and contract awards through the governmentwide point of entry;

4. In the event of equal low bids, awarding first to small business concerns which are also labor surplus area concerns, and second to small business concerns which are not also labor surplus area concerns; and

5. Preparing solicitations that allow the maximum time practicable for response, and furnishing necessary information or explaining where to obtain it, and other related information.

There is no order of precedence among the 8(a) Program, HUBZone Program, Service-Disabled Veteran–Owned Small Business (SDVOSB) Procurement Program, or the Women-Owned Small Business (WOSB). The requirement to exclusively reserve acquisitions for small business concerns at or below the simplified acquisition threshold does not preclude the Contracting Officer from awarding a contract to a small business under the 8(a) Program, HUBZone Program, SDVOSB Program, or WOSB Program.

Above the simplified acquisition threshold, the contracting officer shall first consider an acquisition for the 8(a), HUBZone, SD-VOSB, or WOSB programs before using a small business set-aside. However, if a requirement has been accepted by the SBA under the 8(a) Program, it must remain in the 8(a) Program unless SBA agrees to its release it.

Small business set-asides have priority over acquisitions using full and open competition.

C. Determining North American Industry Classification System (NAICS) codes and Size Standards (FAR 19.303)

The contracting officer shall determine the appropriate NAICS code and related small business size standard and include them in solicitations above the micro-purchase threshold. If different products or services are required in the same solicitation, the solicitation shall identify the appropriate small business size standard for each product or service. The contracting officer's determination is final unless appealed.

If a protest is received that challenges the small business status of an offeror not being considered for award, the contracting officer is not required to suspend contract action. The contracting officer shall forward the protest to the SBA with a notation that the concern is not being considered for award, and shall notify the protester of this action.

An offeror, the SBA, or another interested party may protest the small business representation of an offeror in a specific offer. Any contracting officer who receives a protest, whether timely or not, or who, as the contracting officer, wishes to protest the small business representation of an offeror, or re-representation of a contractor, shall promptly forward the protest to the SBA Government Contracting Area Office for the geographical area where the principal office of the concern in question is located. The protest, or confirmation if the protest was initiated orally, shall be in writing and shall contain the basis for the protest with specific, detailed evidence to support the allegation that the offeror is not small. The SBA will dismiss any protest that does not contain specific grounds for the protest.

In order to affect a specific solicitation, a protest must be timely. To be timely, a protest by any concern or other interested party must be received by the contracting officer by the close of business of the fifth business day after bid opening (for sealed bids) or receipt of the special notification from the contracting officer that identifies the apparently successful offeror (in negotiated acquisitions). A protest may be made orally if it is confirmed in writing either within the five-day period or by letter postmarked no later than one business day after the oral protest. A protest may be made in writing if it is delivered to the contracting officer by hand, telegram, or letter postmarked within the five-day period.

Re-Representation Requirements (FAR 19.301-2 and 10.302(k))

A contractor that represented itself as a small business concern before contract award must re-represent its size status for the NAICS code upon the occurrence of any of the following:

- Within 30 days of execution of a novation agreement or within 30 days after modification of the contract to include the clause 52.219-28 Post-Award Small Business Program Re-representation if the novation agreement was executed prior to inclusion of this clause in the contract;

- Within 30 days after a merger or acquisition of the contractor that does not require a novation or within 30 days after modification of the contract to include the clause 52.219-28 Post-Award Small Business Program Re-representation if the merger or acquisition occurred prior to inclusion of this clause in the contract;

- For long-term contracts,

  ○ Within 60 to 120 days prior to the end of the fifth year of the contract, and

  ○ Within 60 to 120 days prior to the date specified in the contract for exercising any option thereafter.

After a contractor re-represents that it is other than small, the agency may no longer include the value of options exercised, modifications issued, orders issued, or purchases made under BPAs on that contract in its small business prime contracting goal achievements.

A change in size status does not change the terms and conditions of the contract.

D. Cooperation with the Small Business Administration (FAR 19.4)

Under the Small Business Act, the SBA and agencies consult and cooperate to form policies favorable to small business/small disadvantaged business concerns.

SBA procurement center representatives and breakout procurement center representatives review proposed acquisitions for the purpose of recommending set-asides, new sources, and component breakout.

E. Set-Asides for Small Business (FAR 19.5)

In accordance with FAR 19.502-2, small business set-asides have priority over acquisitions using full and open competition. The purpose of small business set-asides is to award certain acquisitions exclusively to small business concerns. Determinations to make a set-aside may be unilateral (made by the contracting officer) or joint (recommended by the SBA procurement center representative and concurred in by the contracting officer). Unilateral determinations are preferred.

Set-asides may be total or partial. Total set-asides are addressed at FAR 19.502-2 while FAR 19.502-3 provides details on partial set-asides. The contracting officer shall set aside a portion of an acquisition that is not subject to simplified acquisition procedures, except for construction, for exclusive small business participation when a total set-aside is not appropriate and the requirement is severable into two or more economic production runs or reasonable lots where one or more small business concerns are expected to have the technical competence and productive capacity to satisfy the set-aside portion of the requirement at a fair market price. A partial set-aside shall not be made if there is a reasonable expectation that only two concerns (one large and one small) with capability will respond with offers unless authorized by the head of a contracting activity on a case-by-case basis. Similarly, a class of acquisitions, not including construction, may be partially set aside. Under certain specified conditions, partial set-asides may be used in conjunction with multiyear contracting procedures.

None of the following is, in itself, sufficient cause for not setting aside an acquisition: a large percentage of previous contracts for the required item(s) have been placed with small business concerns, the item is on a qualified products list, a period of less than 30 days is available for receipt of offers, or the acquisition is classified. (See FAR 19.502-5 for additional insufficient causes for not setting aside an acquisition.)

Contracting officers may reject SBA's set-aside recommendations; however, SBA may appeal. Pending resolution, all action on the acquisition is suspended.

This requirement does not apply to purchases of $3,000 or less ($15,000 or less for acquisitions as described in 13.201(g)(1)), or purchases from required sources of supply under Part 8.

Total Small Business Set-Asides: Each acquisition of supplies or services that has an anticipated dollar value exceeding $3,000 ($15,000 for acquisitions as described in 13.201(g) (1)), but not over $150,000; $300,000 for acquisitions described in paragraph (1) of the Simplified Acquisition Threshold definition at 2.101), is automatically reserved exclusively for small business concerns and shall be set

aside for small business unless the contracting officer determines there is not a reasonable expectation of obtaining offers from two or more responsible small business concerns that are competitive in terms of market prices, quality, and delivery.

The contracting officer shall set aside any acquisition over $150,000 for small business participation when there is a reasonable expectation that offers will be obtained from at least two responsible small business concerns offering the products of different small business concerns, and award will be made at fair market prices.

F. Certificates of Competency and Determination of Responsibility (FAR 19.6)

A Certificate of Competency is the certificate issued by the SBA stating that the holder is responsible (with respect to all elements of responsibility) for the purpose of receiving and performing a specific government contract.

Should a disagreement arise about a concern's ability to perform, the contracting officer and the SBA area office are charged with reaching a resolution; however, if they fail, the matter is referred to the SBA associate administrator for government contracting, who is empowered make the final determination.

G. Statutory Requirements (FAR 19.702)

Statutory Requirements
Any contract that exceeds the simplified acquisition threshold requires the prime contractor to agree that small business concerns, veteran-owned small business concerns, service-disabled veteran–owned small business concerns, HUBZone small business concerns, small disadvantaged business concerns, and woman-owned small business concerns shall have the maximum practicable opportunity to participate in contract performance consistent with its efficient performance.

Solicitations to perform contracts or contract modifications that are expected to exceed $650,000 ($1 million for construction) for which subcontracting possibilities exist, require the apparent successful offeror/bidder to submit an acceptable subcontracting plan prior to award. If the apparently successful offeror fails to negotiate a subcontracting plan acceptable to the Contracting Officer within the time limit prescribed by the Contracting Officer, the offeror will be ineligible for award.

Subcontracting Plans

Contents of an acceptable subcontracting plan are outlined in FAR 19.704. A commercial plan is the preferred type of subcontracting plan for contractors furnishing commercial items. Once a contractor's commercial plan has been approved, the government shall not require another subcontracting plan from the same contractor while the plan remains in effect, as long as the product or service being provided by the contractor continues to meet the definition of a commercial item.

Eligibility Requirements (FAR 19.703)

To be eligible as a subcontractor under the program, a concern must represent itself as a small business, veteran-owned small business, service-disabled veteran–owned small business, HUBZone small business, small disadvantaged business, or woman-owned small business concern. To do so, a concern must meet the appropriate definition.

In connection with a subcontract, or a requirement for which the apparently successful offeror received an evaluation credit for proposing one or more SDB subcontractors, the contracting officer or the SBA may protest the disadvantaged status of a proposed subcontractor. Other interested parties may submit information to the contracting officer or the SBA in an effort to persuade the contracting officer or the SBA to initiate a protest. Such protests, in order to be considered timely, must be submitted to the SBA prior to completion of performance by the intended subcontractor.

A contractor acting in good faith may rely on the written representation of its subcontractor regarding the subcontract's status as a small business, small disadvantaged business, veteran-owned small business, service-disabled veteran-owned small business, or a woman-owned small business concern.

The contractor, the contracting officer or any other interested party may challenge a subcontractor's size status representation.

To implement subcontracting plans, the contractor shall perform the following functions:

- Assist small business concerns so as to facilitate the participation by such concerns;

- Consider use of small business concerns in all "make-or-buy" decisions;

- Counsel and discuss subcontracting opportunities with representatives of small business concerns;

- Confirm that a subcontractor representing itself as a HUBZone small business concern is identified as a certified HUBZone small business concern by accessing the Central Contractor Registration (CCR) database or by contacting SBA;

- Provide notice to subcontractors concerning penalties and remedies for misrepresentations of business status; and

- For all competitive subcontracts over the simplified acquisition threshold in which a small business concern received a small business preference, upon determination of the successful subcontract offeror, the contractor must inform each unsuccessful small business subcontract offeror in writing the name and location of the apparent successful offeror prior to award of the contract.

In making an award that requires a subcontracting plan, the contracting officer shall consider the contractor's compliance with the subcontracting plans submitted on previous contracts as a factor in determining contractor responsibility and assure that a subcontracting plan was submitted when required. The contracting officer shall notify the SBA procurement center representative of the opportunity to review the proposed contract (including the plan and supporting documentation) and shall provide the representative a reasonable time to review the material and submit advisory recommendations, but failure of the representative to respond in a reasonable period of time shall not delay contract award. The contracting officer shall determine any fee that may be payable if an incentive is used in conjunction with the subcontracting plan, and shall ensure that an acceptable plan is incorporated into and made a material part of the contract.

Letter contracts and similar undefinitized instruments, which would otherwise require a subcontracting plan shall contain at least a preliminary basic plan addressing the requirements of 19.704 and in such cases require the negotiation of the final plan within 90 days after award or before definitization, whichever occurs first.

H. Contracting with the Small Business Administration (The 8(a) Program) (FAR 19.8)

Section 8(a) of the Small Business Act established a program that authorizes the SBA to enter into all types of contracts with other agencies and let subcontracts for performing those contracts to firms eligible for program participation. The SBA's subcontractors are referred to as "8(a) contractors."

Contracts may be awarded to the SBA for performance by eligible 8(a) firms on either a sole source or competitive basis.

The SBA and an agency cooperate to match the agency's requirements with the capabilities of 8(a) concerns. The selection of acquisitions for the 8(a) Program is initiated in one of three ways:

1. As a result of a search letter issued by the SBA (this letter advises an agency of an 8(a) firm's capabilities and asks the agency to identify acquisitions to support the firm's business plans);

2. By SBA's identification of a specific agency requirement for a particular 8(a) firm; or

3. By the agency's review of proposed acquisitions for the purpose of identifying requirements that may be offered to the SBA.

I. Status as a Qualified HUBZone Small Business Concern (FAR 19.1303)

The purpose of the Historically Underutilized Business Zone (HUBZone) Program is to provide federal contracting assistance for qualified small business concerns located in historically underutilized business zones, in an effort to increase employment opportunities, investment, and economic development in those areas. If the SBA determines that a concern is a qualified HUBZone small business concern, it will issue a certification to that effect and will add the concern to the List of Qualified HUBZone Small Business Concerns on its website. The concern must appear on the list to be a HUBZone small business concern. The HUBZone procedures apply to all federal agencies that employ one or more contracting officers.

A joint venture may be considered a HUBZone small business concern if it meets the criteria in the explanation of affiliates. A HUBZone small business concern must meet the criteria at the time of its initial offer and at the time of award. (FAR 19.1303(d))

J. The Service-Disabled Veteran–Owned Small Business Procurement Program (FAR 19.14)

The Veterans Benefit Act of 2003 created the procurement program for small business concerns owned and controlled by service-disabled veterans (commonly referred to as the "Service-Disabled Veteran-owned Small Business (SDVOSB) Procurement Program"). The purpose of the Service-Disabled Veteran-Owned Small Business Program is to provide federal contracting assistance to service-disabled veteran–owned small business concerns.

At the time that a service-disabled veteran-owned small business concern submits its offer, it must represent to the contracting officer that it is a service-disabled veteran-owned small business concern and a small business concern under the North American Industry Classification System (NAICS) code assigned to the procurement.

A joint venture may be considered a service-disabled veteran–owned small business concern if

- At least one member of the joint venture is a service-disabled veteran-owned small business concern, and makes the representations in paragraph (b) of this section;

- Each other concern is small under the size standard corresponding to the NAICS code assigned to the procurement;

- The joint venture meets the requirements of an Affiliates; and

- The joint venture meets the requirements of 13 CFR 125.15(b).

The SDVOB procedures apply to all federal agencies that employ one or more contracting officers. The contracting officer may set-aside acquisitions exceeding the micro-purchase threshold for competition restricted to service-disabled veteran–owned small business concerns when the contracting officer has a reasonable expectation that offers will be received from two or more service-disabled veteran–owned small business concerns, and award will be made at a fair market price.

The contracting officer shall consider service-disabled veteran-owned small business set-asides before considering service-disabled veteran-owned small business sole source awards.

K. Women-Owned Small Business (WOSB) Program (FAR 19.15)

The purpose of the WOSB Program is to ensure women-owned small business concerns have an equal opportunity to participate in federal contracting and to assist agencies in achieving their WOSB participation goals.

Status
- Status as an economically disadvantaged women-owned small business (ED-WOSB) or WOSB concern is determined in accordance with 13 CFR Part 127.

- The contracting officer shall verify that the offeror

  o Is registered in Central Contractor Registration (CCR);

  o Is self-certified in the Online Representation and Certifications Application (ORCA); and

  o Has submitted documents verifying its eligibility at the time of initial offer to the WOSB Program Repository. The contract shall not be awarded until all required documents are received.

- Certification by an SBA-approved certifier:

  o An EDWOSB or WOSB concern that has been certified by an SBA approved third party certifier, (which includes

SBA certification under the 8(a) Program), must provide the following eligibility requirement documents: the third-party certification; SBA's WOSB Program Certification form (SBA Form 2413); and the joint venture agreement, if applicable.

° An EDWOSB or WOSB concern that has not been certified by an SBA approved third party certifier or by SBA under the 8(a) Program, must provide the following documents documentation required by FAR 19.1503(c)(2):

Set-aside Procedures

The contracting officer may set aside acquisitions exceeding the micro-purchase threshold for competition restricted to EDWOSB or WOSB concerns eligible under the WOSB Program in those NAICS codes in which SBA has determined that women-owned small business concerns are underrepresented or substantially underrepresented in Federal procurement, as specified on SBA's Web site at **www.sba.gov/WOSB**.

For requirements in NAICS codes designated by SBA as **underrepresented**, a contracting officer may restrict competition to EDWOSB concerns if the contracting officer has a reasonable expectation based on market research that

- Two or more EDWOSB concerns will submit offers for the contract;

- The anticipated award price of the contract (including options) does not exceed $6.5 million, in the case of a contract assigned an NAICS code for manufacturing; or $4 million, for all other contracts; and

- Contract award will be made at a fair and reasonable price.

A contracting officer may restrict competition to WOSB concerns eligible under the WOSB Program (including EDWOSB concerns),

for requirements in NAICS codes designated by SBA as **substantially underrepresented** if there is a reasonable expectation based on market research that

- Two or more WOSB concerns (including EDWOSB concerns) will submit offers;

- The anticipated award price of the contract (including options) will not exceed $6.5 million, in the case of a contract assigned an NAICS code for manufacturing, or $4 million for all other contracts; and

- Contract award may be made at a fair and reasonable price.

The contracting officer may make an award, if only one acceptable offer is received from a qualified EDWOSB or WOSB concern.

The contracting officer must check whether the apparently successful offeror filed all the required eligibility documents, and file a status protest if any documents are missing. (FAR 19.1503(d)(2))

If no acceptable offers are received from an EDWOSB or WOSB concern, the set-aside shall be withdrawn and the requirement, if still valid, must be considered for set aside in accordance with 19.203 and subpart 19.5.

FAR Part 22. Application of Labor Laws to Government Acquisitions

A. Basic Labor Policies (FAR 22.1)

Agencies are required to maintain sound relations with industry and labor to ensure prompt receipt of information involving labor relations that may adversely affect the government acquisition process and to ensure that the government obtains needed supplies and services without delay.

Agencies shall remain impartial concerning any dispute between labor and contractor management and not undertake the conciliation, mediation, or arbitration of a labor dispute. To the extent practicable, agencies should ensure that the parties to the dispute use all available methods for resolving the dispute, including the services of the National Labor Relations Board; Federal Mediation and Conciliation Service; the National Mediation Board; and other appropriate federal, state, local, or private agencies.

The head of the contracting activity may designate programs or requirements for which it is necessary that contractors be required to notify the government of actual or potential labor disputes that are delaying or threaten to delay timely contract performance.

Agencies are to cooperate and encourage contractors to cooperate with federal and state agencies responsible for enforcing labor requirements.

"Normal workweek" generally means a workweek of 40 hours. "Overtime" means time worked by a contractor's employee in excess of the employee's normal workweek.

Contractors are required to perform all government contracts, so far as practicable, without using overtime, except when lower overall costs to the government will result or when it is necessary to meet urgent program needs.

B. Contract Work Hours and Safety Standards Act (FAR 22.3)

No laborer or mechanic shall be required or permitted to work more than 40 hours a week unless paid time and a half.

The act is applicable to contracts that may require or involve the employment of laborers or mechanics.

C. Labor Standards for Contracts Involving Construction (FAR 22.4)

Applicable to contracts >$2,000, for construction, alteration, or repair, including painting and decorating, of public buildings and public works.

The Davis-Bacon Act provides that no laborer or mechanic employed on the site shall receive less than prevailing wage rates as determined by the Secretary of Labor.

The Copeland (Anti-Kickback) Act makes it unlawful to induce any person to give up any part of the compensation to which that person is entitled under a contract of employment.

The Contract Work Hours and Safety Standards Act requires that laborers and mechanics must be paid time and a half for overtime work (>40 hrs per week).

Wage determinations are discussed in FAR 22.404-1 through 11. There are two types: general (prevailing wage rates within a specified geographical area, no expiration date); and project (specific to project, used when no general wage determination applies, effective for 180 calendar days). Once incorporated in a contract, wage determinations normally remain effective for the life of the contract.

Contracting agencies are responsible for enforcing labor standards in the administration of construction contracts. This is most commonly done through review of payrolls and statements and regular compliance checks. Results are then reported to the Department of Labor through the submission of semiannual enforcement reports.

D. Project Labor Agreements (FAR 22.5)

A project labor agreement (PLA) is a pre-hire collective bargaining agreement with one or more labor organizations that establishes the terms and conditions of employment for a specific construction project. PLAs allow all contractors and subcontractors to compete on the project without regard to whether they are otherwise parties to collective bargaining agreements, contain guarantees against strikes, lockouts and similar job disruptions, establish procedures for resolving labor disputes and provide other mechanisms for labor-management cooperation.

If appropriate, an agency may require that every contractor and subcontractor engaged in a construction project greater than $25 million agree, for that project, become a party to a PLA with one or more labor organizations.

Agencies may consider the following factors in deciding whether the use of a PLA is appropriate:

- The project will require multiple construction contractors and/or subcontractors employing workers in multiple crafts or trades;

- The possibility of a shortage of skilled labor in the region in which the construction project will be sited;

- Completion of the project will require an extended period of time;

- PLAs have been used on comparable projects in the geographic area of the project;

- A PLA will promote the agency's long term program interests, such as facilitating the training of a skilled workforce to meet the agency's future construction needs; and

- Any other factors that the agency decides are appropriate.

E. Walsh-Healey Public Contracts Act (FAR 22.6)

The act applies to supply contracts valued in excess of $15,000. It addresses such matters as minimum wages, maximum hours, child labor, convict labor, and safe and sanitary working conditions.

Statutory/regulatory exemptions are listed in FAR 22.604-1 and -2.

F. Equal Employment Opportunity (FAR 22.8)

Required in all nonexempt governmental prime and subcontracts to promote equal employment opportunities for all persons, regardless of race, color, religion, sex, or national origin. See FAR 22.807 for exemptions.

Contractors found to be in violation are subject to having their names or the names of their unions published; cancellation, termination, or suspension of the contract; debarment; and referral to the Department of Justice or EEO Commission for civil or criminal proceedings.

G. Service Contract Act of 1965, As Amended (FAR 22.10)

Service contracts valued in excess of $2,500 must contain mandatory provisions regarding minimum wage and fringe benefits, safe and sanitary working conditions, notification to employees of the minimum allowable compensation, and equivalent federal employee classifications and wage rates. Statutory exemptions are covered in FAR 22.1003-3.

Contracting officers may obtain wage determinations using the WDOL website or the Department of Labor's e98 electronic process. Contracting officers must include the applicable wage determination in the solicitation and resulting contract.

FAR Part 23. Environment, Energy and Water Efficiency, Renewable Energy Technologies, Occupational Safety, and Drug-Free Workplace

This part prescribes policies and procedures supporting the government's program for ensuring a drug-free workplace, occupational safety and for protecting and improving the quality of the environment by

- Controlling pollution;

- Managing energy and water use in government facilities efficiently;

- Using renewable energy and renewable energy technologies;

- Acquiring energy- and water-efficient products and services, environmentally preferable products, and products that use recovered materials and bio-based products;

- Requiring contractors to identify hazardous materials.

- Encouraging contractors to adopt and enforce policies that ban text messaging while driving; and

- Requiring contractors to comply with agency environmental management systems.

A. Energy and Water Efficiency and Renewable Energy (FAR 23.2)

The government's policy is to acquire supplies and services that promote energy and water efficiency, advance the use of renewable energy products, and help foster markets for emerging technologies. This policy extends to all acquisitions, including those below the simplified acquisition threshold.

B. Use of Recovered Materials and Bio-based Products (FAR 23.4)

The Resource Conservation and Recovery Act of 1976 (RCRA), 42 U.S.C. 6962, requires agencies responsible for drafting or reviewing specifications used in agency acquisitions to eliminate from those specifications any requirement excluding the use of recovered materials or requiring products to be manufactured from virgin materials; and require, for EPA-designated products, using recovered materials and bio-based products to the maximum extent practicable without jeopardizing the intended end use of the item.

Government policy on the use of products containing recovered materials and bio-based products considers cost, availability of competition, and performance. The objective is to acquire competitively, in a cost-effective manner, products that meet reasonable performance requirements and that are composed of the highest percentage of recovered materials practicable.

C. Drug-Free Workplace (FAR 23.5)

No offeror other than an individual shall be considered a responsible source (see 9.104-1(g) and 19.602-1(a)(2)(i)) for a contract that exceeds the simplified acquisition threshold, unless it agrees that it will provide a drug-free workplace by publishing a statement notifying its employees that the unlawful manufacture, distribution, dispensing, possession, or use of a controlled substance is prohibited in the contractor's workplace, and specifying the actions that will be taken against employees for violations of such prohibition and establishing an ongoing drug-free awareness program.

D. Contracting for Environmentally Preferable and Energy Efficient Products and Services (FAR 23.7)

Agencies must implement cost-effective contracting preference programs promoting energy-efficiency, water conservation, and the acquisition of environmentally preferable products and services; and employ acquisition strategies that maximize the utilization of environmentally preferable products and services (based on EPA-issued guidance); promote energy-efficiency and water conservation; eliminate or reduce the generation of hazardous waste and the need for special material processing (including special handling, storage, treatment, and disposal); promote the use of nonhazardous and recovered materials; promote the use of bio-based products; and realize life-cycle cost savings.

E. Contractor Compliance with Environmental Management Systems (FAR 23.9)

An environmental management system (EMS) is a set of processes and practices that enable an organization to reduce its environmental impacts and to increase its operating efficiency. Where contractor activities affect the environmental management performance of the agency, the Contracting Officer is required to specify the EMS directives with which the contractor must comply, and to ensure contractor compliance to the same extent as the agency would be required to comply, if the agency operated the facilities or vehicles.

FAR Part 24. Protection of Privacy and Freedom of Information

This part prescribes policies and procedures that apply requirements of the Privacy Act of 1974 and cites the Freedom of Information Act.

A. Protection of Individual Privacy (FAR 24.1)

The Privacy Act requires that when an agency contracts for the design, development, or operation of a system of records on individuals on behalf of the agency to accomplish an agency function the agency must apply the requirements of the act to the contractor and its employees working on the contract. An agency officer or employee may be criminally liable for violations of the Privacy Act.

B. Freedom of Information Act (FAR 24.2)

The Freedom of Information Act (5 U.S.C. 552, as amended) provides that information is to be made available to the public either by

- Publication in the *Federal Register*;

- Providing an opportunity to read and copy records at convenient locations; or

- Upon request, providing a copy of a reasonably described record.

The act specifies, among other things, how agencies shall make their records available upon public request, imposes strict time standards for agency responses, and exempts certain records from public disclosure.

A proposal submitted in response to a competitive solicitation, shall not be made available to any person under the Freedom of Information Act. This prohibition does not apply to a proposal, or any part of a proposal, that is set forth or incorporated by reference in a contract between the Government and the contractor that submitted the proposal.

Contracting officers may receive requests for records that may be exempted from mandatory public disclosure. The exemptions most often applicable are those relating to classified information, to trade secrets and confidential commercial or financial information, to interagency or intra-agency memoranda, or to personal and medical information pertaining to an individual. Since these requests often involve complex issues requiring an in-depth knowledge of a large and increasing body of court rulings and policy guidance, contracting officers are cautioned to comply with the implementing regulations of their agency and to obtain necessary guidance from the agency officials having Freedom of Information Act responsibility. If additional assistance is needed, authorized agency officials may contact the Department of Justice, Office of Information and Privacy.

FAR Part 25. Foreign Acquisition

This part provides policies and procedures for the acquisition of foreign supplies, services, and construction materials and contracts performed outside the United States. It also implements the Buy American Act, trade agreements, and other laws and regulations.

A. Buy American Act–Supplies (FAR 25.1)

The Buy American Act restricts the purchase of supplies that are not domestic end products. A foreign end product may be purchased if the contracting officer determines that the price of the lowest domestic offer is unreasonable or if another exception applies. For manufactured end products, the Buy American Act uses a two-part test to define a domestic end product. The article must be manufactured in the United States and the cost of domestic components must exceed 50 percent of the cost of all components.

B. Buy American Act– Construction Materials (FAR 25.2)

The Buy American Act requires that only domestic construction materials be used in construction contracts performed in the United States. Exceptions to the act are found at FAR 25.202.

The contracting officer must review allegations of Buy American Act violations and when necessary, take appropriate action such as process a determination concerning the inapplicability of the Buy American Act in accordance with 25.205; consider requiring the removal and replacement of the unauthorized foreign construction material; or determine in writing that the material need not be removed because it would be detrimental to the interests of the government. If the noncompliance is sufficiently serious, consider exercising appropriate contractual remedies, such as terminating the contract for default or forwarding a report to the agency suspension or debarring official.

C. Trade Agreements (FAR 25.4)

The trade agreements waive the applicability of the Buy American Act for some foreign supplies and construction materials from certain countries. Free Trade Agreements and the World Trade Organization (WTO) Government Procurement Agreement specify procurement procedures designed to ensure fairness. The value of the acquisition is a determining factor in the applicability of the trade agreements. When the restrictions of the Buy American Act are waived for eligible products, offers of those products (eligible offers) receive equal consideration with domestic offers. Under the Trade Agreements Act, only United States–made end products or eligible products may be acquired (also see 25.403(c)). FAR 25.402 lists the applicable thresholds. See Subpart 25.5 for evaluation procedures for supply contracts subject to trade agreements. The dollar thresholds are subject to revision every two years.

FAR Part 27. Patents, Data, and Copyrights

Part 27 covers patents, data, and copyrights and applies to all agencies. However, agencies are authorized to adopt alternative policies, procedures, solicitation provisions, and contract clauses to the extent necessary to meet the specific requirements of laws, executive orders, treaties, or international agreements.

As with many areas of the *FAR*, this part is extremely complex and has many nuances associated with is application in contracts and in industry. The information in this guide is meant as a summary, and any specific questions or detailed issues should be referred to a specialist in this field.

A. General (FAR Part 27.1)

The government encourages the maximum practical commercial use of inventions made under government contracts. Generally, the government will not refuse to award a contract on the grounds that the prospective contractor may infringe a patent. The government may authorize and consent to the use of inventions in the performance of certain contracts, even though the inventions may be covered by U.S. patents. Generally, contractors providing commercial items should indemnify the government against liability of the infringement of U.S. patents. The government recognizes rights in data developed at private expense, and limits its demands for delivery of that data. When such data is delivered, the government will acquire only those rights essential to its needs. The government requires that contractors obtain permission from copyright owners before including copyrighted works, owned by others, in data to be delivered to the government.

B. Patents and Copyrights (FAR Part 27.2)

The exclusive remedy for patent or copyright infringement by or on behalf of the government is a suit for monetary damages against the government in the Court of Federal Claims. There is no injunctive relief available, and there is no direct cause of action against a contractor that is infringing a patent or copyright with the authorization or consent of the government (e.g., while performing a contract). The government may expressly authorize and consent to a contractor's use or manufacture of inventions covered by U.S. patents by inserting the clause at 52.227-1, Authorization and Consent.

Because of the exclusive remedies granted in 28 U.S.C. 1498, the government requires notice and assistance from its contractors regarding any claims for patent or copyright infringement by inserting the clause at 52.227-2, Notice and Assistance, Regarding Patent, and Copyright Infringement. The government may require a contractor to reimburse it for liability for patent infringement arising out of a contract for commercial items by inserting the clause at FAR 52.227-3, Patent Indemnity.

Prospective contractors are required to furnish royalty information in proposals so the contracting officer can determine whether royalties anticipated or actually paid under government contracts are excessive, improper, or inconsistent with government patent rights. The contracting officer shall take appropriate action to reduce or eliminate excessive or improper royalties. If the response to a solicitation includes a charge for royalties, the contracting officer shall, before award of the contract, forward the information to the office having cognizance of patent matters for the contracting activity. The cognizant office shall promptly advise the contracting officer of appropriate action.

The contracting officer, when considering the approval of a subcontract, shall require royalty information if it is required under the prime contract. The contracting officer shall forward the information to the office having cognizance of patent matters. However, the contracting officer need not delay consent while awaiting advice from the cognizant office.

The contracting officer shall forward any royalty reports to the office having cognizance of patent matters for the contracting activity.

If at any time the contracting officer believes that any royalties paid, or to be paid, under a contract or subcontract are inconsistent with government rights, excessive, or otherwise improper, the contracting officer shall promptly report the facts to the office having cognizance of patent matters for the contracting activity concerned. In coordination with the cognizant office, the contracting officer shall promptly act to protect the government against payment of royalties where the government has a royalty-free license, where the rate is in excess of the government license, or where the royalties in whole or in part constitute an improper charge,

Unauthorized disclosure of classified subject matter, whether in patent applications or resulting from the issuance of a patent, may be a violation of 18 U.S.C. 792, et seq. (Chapter 37–Espionage and Censorship), and related statutes, and may be contrary to the interests of national security. To prevent such disclosures, upon receipt of a patent application the contracting officer shall ascertain the proper security classification of the patent application. If the application contains classified subject matter, the contracting officer shall inform the contractor how to transmit the application to the U.S. Patent Office in accordance with procedures provided by legal counsel. If the material is classified "Secret" or higher, the contracting officer shall make every effort to notify the contractor within 30 days of the government's determination. Upon receipt of information furnished by the contractor the contracting officer shall promptly submit that information to legal counsel in order that the steps necessary to ensure the security of the application will be taken. The contracting Officer shall act promptly on requests for approval of foreign filing in order to avoid the loss of valuable patent rights of the government or the contractor.

With respect to patented technology covered under trade agreements, there are specific notice requirements when the patent holder is from a country that is a party to the North American Free Trade Agreement (NAFTA). Article 1709(10) of NAFTA generally requires a user of technology covered by a valid patent to make a reasonable effort to obtain authorization prior to use of the patented technology. However, NAFTA provides that this requirement for authorization may be waived in situations of national emergency or other circumstances of extreme urgency, or for public noncommercial use. Section 6 of Executive Order 12889, "Implementation of the North American Free Trade Act," of December 27, 1993, waives the requirement to obtain advance authorization for an invention used or manufactured by or for the federal government.

C. Patent Rights under Government Contracts (FAR Part 27.3)

It is the policy and objective of the government to use the patent system to promote the use of inventions arising from federally supported research or development; and to encourage maximum participation of industry in federally supported research and development efforts. It is in the government's interest to ensure that these inventions are used in a manner to promote free competition and enterprise without unduly encumbering future research and discovery as well as ensuring that the government retains sufficient rights in these inventions to meet its needs and protect the public against unreasonable use or nonuse while minimizing the cost of administering patents and their policies. It is highly desirable to promote the commercialization and public availability of the inventions made in the United States by United States industry and labor.

Generally, each contractor may, after required disclosure to the government, elect to retain title to any subject invention.

Exceptions to this general policy exist and are fully documented in the FAR Part 27-3. These exceptions generally occur when contractors are outside the U.S. or there are issues or concerns relating to foreign governments or national security, particularly with respect to nuclear programs. However, even when the government has the right to acquire title to a subject invention, the contractor may nevertheless request greater rights.

The government shall have at least a nonexclusive, nontransferable, irrevocable, paid-up license to practice, or have practiced for or on behalf of the United States, any subject invention throughout the world. The government may require additional rights in order to comply with treaties or other international agreements. In such case, these rights shall be made a part of the contract.

Pursuant to 35 U.S.C. 203, agencies have certain march-in rights that require the contractor, an assignee, or exclusive licensee of a subject invention to grant a nonexclusive, partially exclusive, or exclusive license in any field of use to responsible applicants, upon terms that are reasonable under the circumstances. If the contractor, assignee or exclusive licensee of a subject invention refuses to grant such a license, the agency can grant the license itself. March-in rights may be exercised only if the agency determines that this action is necessary.

When the government acquires title to a subject invention, the contractor is normally granted a revocable, nonexclusive, paid-up license to that subject invention throughout the world. The contractor's license extends to any of its domestic subsidiaries and affiliates. The contracting officer shall approve or disapprove, in writing, any contractor request to transfer its licenses.

Publishing information concerning an invention before a patent application is filed on a subject invention may create a bar to a valid patent. To avoid this bar, agencies may withhold information from the public that discloses any invention in which the government owns or may own a right, title, or interest (including a nonexclusive license). Agencies may only withhold information concerning inventions for a reasonable time in order for a patent application to be filed. Once filed in any patent office, agencies are not required to release copies of any document that is a part of a patent application for those subject inventions.

D. Rights in Data and Copyrights (FAR Part 27.4)

All contracts that require data to be produced, furnished, acquired or used in meeting contract performance requirements, must contain terms that delineate the respective rights and obligations of the government and the contractor regarding the use, reproduction, and disclosure of that data. Data rights clauses do not specify the type, quantity or quality of data that is to be delivered, but only the respective rights of the government and the contractor regarding the use, disclosure, or reproduction of the data. Accordingly, the contract shall specify the data to be delivered.

The government acquires unlimited rights in the following data, except for copyrighted works:

- Data first produced in the performance of a contract (except to the extent the data constitute minor modifications to data that are limited rights data or restricted computer software);

- Form, fit, and function data delivered under contract;

- Data (except as may be included with restricted computer software) that constitute manuals or instructional and training material for installation, operation, or routine maintenance and repair of items, components, or processes delivered or furnished for use under a contract; and

- All other data delivered under the contract other than limited rights data or restricted computer software. (FAR 27.404-2)

The basic clause at FAR 52.227-14, Rights in Data—General, enables the contractor to protect qualifying limited rights data and restricted computer software by withholding the data from the government and instead delivering form, fit, and function data.

For contracts that do not require the development, use, or delivery of items, components, or processes that are intended to be acquired by or for the government, an agency may adopt the alternate definition of limited rights data set forth in Alternate I to the clause at FAR 52.227-14. The alternate definition does not require that the data pertain to items, components, or processes developed at private expense; but rather that the data were developed at private expense and embody a trade secret or are commercial or financial and confidential or privileged.

The clause at FAR 52.227-14 with its Alternate II enables the government to require delivery of limited rights data rather than allow the contractor to withhold the data. Alternate III of the clause at FAR 52.227-14, enables the government to require delivery of restricted computer software rather than allow the contractor to withhold such restricted computer software.

Generally, the contractor must obtain permission of the contracting officer prior to asserting rights in any copyrighted work containing data first produced in the performance of a contract. However, contractors are normally authorized, without prior approval of the contracting officer, to assert copyright in technical or scientific articles based on or containing such data that is published in academic, technical or professional journals, symposia proceedings, and similar works. There are alternate versions of the contract clause that permit various usage, and the most appropriate one should be selected. Contractors shall not deliver any data that is not first produced under the contract without either acquiring for or granting to the government a copyright license for the data or obtaining permission from the contracting officer to do otherwise.

Data delivered to the government with any restrictions on its use must be marked correctly and conspicuously. The government may reject any data delivered to it that is incorrectly marked.

FAR Part 28. Bonds and Insurance

This part prescribes requirements for obtaining financial protection against losses under contracts that result from the use of the sealed bid or negotiated methods. It covers bid guarantees, bonds, alternative payment protections, security for bonds, and insurance.

A. Definitions (FAR 28.001)

Bid guarantee means a form of security ensuring that the bidder will not withdraw a bid within the period specified for acceptance and will execute a written contract and furnish required bonds, within the allotted time following award.

A *bond* is a written instrument executed by a bidder or contractor (the principal), and a second party (the surety) (except as provided in 28.204), to ensure fulfillment of the principal's obligations to a third party (the obligee or government), identified in the bond. If the principal's obligations are not met, the bond assures payment, to the extent stipulated, of any loss sustained by the obligee.

Bond Types
- Advance payment bond—secures fulfillment of the contractor's obligations under an advance payment provision);

- Annual bid bond—a single bond, in lieu of separate bonds, which secures all bids on other than construction contracts requiring bonds submitted during a specific fiscal year;

- Annual performance bond—a single bond, in lieu of separate performance bonds, to secure fulfillment of the contractor's obligations under contracts other than for construction requiring bonds entered into during a specific fiscal year;

- Patent infringement bond—secures fulfillment of the contractor's obligations under a patent provision;

- Payment bond—ensures payments as required by law to all persons supplying labor or material in the prosecution of the work provided for in the contract; and

- Performance bond—secures performance and fulfillment of the contractor's obligations under the contract.

Surety means an individual or corporation legally liable for the debt, default, or failure of a principal to satisfy a contractual obligation. There are three types:

- Individual—one person, versus a business entity, who is liable for the entire penal amount of the bond;

- Corporate—licensed under various insurance laws, and under its charter, has legal power to act as surety for others; and

- Co-surety—one of two or more sureties that are jointly liable for the penal sum of the bond.

Insurance means a contract that provides that for a stipulated consideration, one party undertakes to indemnify another against loss, damage, or liability arising from an unknown or contingent event.

B. Bonds and Other Financial Protections (FAR 28.1)

A contracting officer shall not require a bid guarantee unless a performance bond or a performance and payment bond is also required. In sealed bidding, noncompliance with a solicitation requirement for a bid guarantee requires rejection of the bid except for those situations described in FAR 28.101-4(c).

The Miller Act requires performance and payment bonds for any construction contract valued in excess of $150,000, unless waived. Generally, such bonds are not required for other than construction contracts; however, in some situations, performance bonds may be appropriate. (FAR 28.103-2(a) 1-4)

Performance bonds secure performance and fulfillment of the contractor's obligations under the contract. They may be required for contracts exceeding the simplified acquisition threshold when necessary to protect the government's interest. Situations that may warrant a performance bond are delineated in FAR 28.103-2. Unless the contracting officer determines that a lesser amount is adequate for the protection of the government, the penal amount of performance bonds must equal to 100 percent of the original contract price; and if the contract price increases, an additional amount equal to 100 percent of the increase.

Payment bonds ensure payment as required by law to all persons supplying labor or materials in the prosecution of the work provided for in the contact. They are required only when a performance bond is required and it is determined to be in the government's best interest to use them. Penal amounts are determined by the contracting officer.

C. Alternatives in Lieu of Corporate or Individual Sureties (FAR 28.204)

Any person required to furnish a bond to the government may furnish any of the following types of securities instead of a corporate or individual surety for the bond: U.S. bonds or notes; certified or cashier's checks, bank drafts, money orders, or currency; or an irrevocable letter of credit (ILC).

The contractor must furnish all bonds or alternative payment protection, including any necessary reinsurance agreements, before receiving a notice to proceed with the work or being allowed to start work.

D. Sureties and Other Security for Bonds (FAR 28.2)

Surety means an individual or corporation legally liable for the debt, default, or failure of a principal to satisfy a contractual obligation. There are three types: individual, corporate, and co-surety (one of two or more sureties that are jointly liable for the penal sum of the bond).

Agencies are required to obtain adequate security for bonds required or used with a contract. Acceptable forms of security include corporate or individual sureties or any of the types of security authorized in lieu of sureties, (i.e., United States bonds or notes, certified or cashier's checks, bank drafts, Post Office money orders, or currency, or an irrevocable letter of credit).

E. Insurance (FAR 28.3)

The government requires any contractor subject to CAS 416 to obtain insurance, by purchase or self-coverage, except when the government agrees to indemnify the contractor under specified circumstances or the contract specifically relieves the contractor of liability for loss or damage to government property.

Contractors, whether or not subject to CAS 416, are required by law and the *FAR* to provide certain types of insurance, (e.g., workers compensation). Insurance is also required when commingling of property, type of operation, circumstances of ownership, or condition of the contract make it necessary for the protection of the government.

FAR Part 29. Taxes

A. Federal Excise Taxes (FAR 29.2)

Federal excise taxes are levied on the sale or use of particular supplies and services. Contracting officers should solicit prices on a tax-exclusive basis when it is known that the government is exempt from these taxes, and on a tax-inclusive basis when no exemption exists.

B. State and Local Taxes (FAR 29.3)

Generally, purchases and leases made by the federal government are immune from state and local taxation. Whether any specific purchase or lease is immune is a legal question

requiring advice and assistance of the agency-designated counsel. When it is economically feasible to do so, executive agencies shall take maximum advantage of all available exemptions. If appropriate, the contracting officer shall provide a Standard Form 1094, U.S. Tax Exemption Form, to establish that the purchase is being made by the government.

Prime contractors and subcontractors shall not normally be designated as agents of the government for the purpose of claiming immunity from state or local sales or use taxes.

FAR Part 30. The Cost Accounting Standards (CAS) Administration

A. Cost Accounting Standards (FAR 30.1)

Public Law 100-679 (41 U.S.C. 422) requires certain contractors and subcontractors to comply with Cost Accounting Standards (CAS) and to disclose in writing and follow consistently their cost accounting practices.

B. CAS Program Requirements (FAR 30.2)

The contracting officer is responsible for determining when a proposed contract may require CAS coverage and for including the appropriate notice in the solicitation. The contracting officer must then ensure that the offeror has made the required solicitation certifications and that required disclosure statements are submitted.

The contracting officer shall not award a CAS-covered contract until the cognizant federal agency official (CFAO) has made a written determination that a required disclosure statement is adequate unless, in order to protect the government's interest, the agency head authorizes award without obtaining the required disclosure statement. In this event, a determination of adequacy shall be required as soon as possible after the award.

The head of the agency may waive the applicability of CAS for a particular contract or subcontract when either of the following situations exists:

- The contract or subcontract value is less than $15,000,000, the segment of the contractor or subcontractor that will perform the contract or subcontract is primarily engaged in the sale of commercial items, and has no contracts or subcontracts that are subject to CAS; or

- Exceptional circumstances exist whereby a waiver of CAS is necessary to meet the needs of the agency. Exceptional circumstances exist only when the benefits to be derived from waiving the CAS outweigh the risk associated with the waiver. The determination that exceptional circumstances exist must be set forth in writing; and include a statement of the specific circumstances that justify granting the waiver.

C. CAS Administration (FAR 30.6)

This subpart describes policies and procedures for applying the Cost Accounting Standards Board (CASB) rules and regulations (48 CFR Chapter 99 (*FAR* Appendix)) to negotiated contracts and subcontracts. It does not apply to sealed bid contracts or to any contract with a small business concern. (See 48 CFR 9903.201-1(b) (FAR Appendix) for these and other exemptions.)

The CFAO shall perform CAS administration for all contracts and subcontracts in a business unit notwithstanding retention of other administration functions by the contracting officer. Within 30 days after the award of any new contract or subcontract subject to CAS, the contracting officer, contractor, or subcontractor making the award shall request the cognizant ACO to perform administration for CAS matters.

D. Changes to Disclosed or Established Cost Accounting Practices (FAR 30.603)

Required Changes: Offerors shall state whether the award of a contract would require a change to an established cost accounting practice affecting existing contracts and subcontracts (see FAR 52.230-1). The contracting officer shall notify the CFAO if the offeror states that a change in cost accounting practice would be required.

Unilateral Changes: The contractor may unilaterally change its disclosed or established cost accounting practices, but the government shall not pay any increased cost, in the aggregate, as a result of the unilateral change.

Desirable Changes: Prior to taking action under the applicable paragraph(s) addressing a desirable change at 52.230-2, 52.230-3, or 52.230-5, the CFAO shall determine that the change is a desirable change and not detrimental to the interests of the government. Until the CFAO has determined that a change to a cost accounting practice is a desirable change, the change is a unilateral change. Some factors to consider in determining if a change is desirable include, but are not limited to, whether

1. The contractor must change the cost accounting practices it uses for government contract and subcontract costing purposes to remain in compliance with the provisions of Part 31;

2. The contractor is initiating management actions directly associated with the change that will result in cost savings for segments with CAS-covered contracts and subcontracts over a period for which forward pricing rates are developed or five years, whichever is shorter, and the cost savings are reflected in the forward pricing rates; and

3. Funds are available if the determination would necessitate an upward adjustment of contract cost or price.

This part contains cost principles and procedures for pricing contracts, subcontracts, and modifications to contracts and subcontracts whenever cost analysis is performed and determination, negotiation, or allowance of costs when required by a contract clause.

Contractors needing assistance in developing or improving their accounting systems and procedures may request a copy of the *Defense Contract Audit Agency Pamphlet No. 7641.90, Information for Contractors* at **www.dcaa.mil**.

Definitions (FAR 31.001): This section contains numerous definitions that are used in this part, and FAR 31.001 can be marked for quick reference to these terms. Some terms of particular note are listed below.

A. Fixed-Price Contracts (FAR 31.1)

Application of cost principles to fixed-price contracts and subcontracts shall not be construed as a requirement to negotiate agreements on individual elements of cost in arriving at agreement on total price. The final price accepted by the parties reflects agreement only on the total price. Further, notwithstanding the mandatory use of cost principles, the objective will continue to be to negotiate prices that are fair and reasonable, cost and other factors considered.

Advance agreements may be negotiated either before or during a contract, but should be negotiated before incurrence of the costs involved. The agreements must be in writing, executed by both contracting parties, and incorporated into applicable current and future contracts. Advance agreements may be negotiated with a particular contractor for a single contract, a group of contracts, or all the contracts of a contracting office, an agency, or several agencies

B. Contracts with Commercial Organizations (FAR 31.2)

The total cost of a contract is the sum of the direct and indirect costs allocable to the contract, incurred or to be incurred, less any allocable credits, plus any allocable cost of money. While the total cost of a contract includes all cost properly allocable to the contract using any equitable method that is consistently applied, the allowable costs to the government are limited to those allocable costs allowable pursuant to Part 31 and applicable agency supplements. Factors to be considered in determining whether a cost is allowable include reasonableness, allocability, generally accepted accounting principles and practices or standards promulgated by the CAS Board, and terms of the contract.

A cost is reasonable if, in its nature and amount, it does not exceed that which would be incurred by a prudent person in the conduct of competitive business. A cost is allocable if it is assignable or chargeable to one or more cost objectives on the basis of relative benefits received or other equitable relationship. Subject to the foregoing, a cost is allocable to a government contract if it is incurred specifically for the contract, benefits both the contract and other work, and can be distributed to them in reasonable proportion to the benefits received, or is necessary to the overall operation of the business, although a direct relationship to any particular cost objective cannot be shown.

Interest on borrowings (however represented), bond discounts, costs of financing and refinancing capital, legal and professional fees paid in connection with preparing prospectuses, and costs of preparing and issuing stock rights are unallowable. However, interest assessed by state or local taxing authorities under the conditions specified in 31.205-41(a)(3) is allowable.

This *FAR* subpart contains several types of costs and prescribes specific guidelines for their treatment under government contracts. The *FAR* should be consulted for specific guidance.

C. Contracts with Educational Institutions (FAR 31.3)

This *FAR* subpart references the appropriate OMB circular detailing cost treatment for contracts with educational institutions. Agencies are not expected to place additional restrictions on individual items of cost.

D. Contracts with State, Locally, and Federally Recognized Indian Tribal Governments (FAR 31.6)

Similar to the previous section, an OMB circular details specific cost treatment for these specialized contracts. While agencies are not expected to place additional restrictions on individual cost items, this clause requires that certain types of costs be treated as unallowable.

E. Contracts with Nonprofit Organizations (FAR 31.7)

This FAR subpart references the appropriate OMB circular detailing cost treatment for contracts with nonprofit organizations. Agencies are not expected to place additional restrictions on individual items of cost.

FAR Part 32. Contract Financing

This part prescribes policies and procedures for contract financing and other payment matters. This includes

- Payment methods, including partial payments and progress payments based on percentage or stage of completion;

- Loan guarantees, advance payments, and progress payments based on costs;

- Administration of debts to the government arising out of contracts;

- Contract funding, including the use of contract clauses limiting costs or funds;

- Assignment of claims to aid in private financing;

- Selected payment clauses;

- Financing of purchases of commercial items;

- Performance-based payments; and

- Electronic funds transfer payments.

A. Non-Commercial Item Purchase Financing (FAR 32.1)

Government financing is to be provided only to the extent actually needed for prompt and efficient performance, considering the availability of private financing. Contract financing is intended to be self-liquidating through contract performance; consequently, agencies may finance contractor working capital, but not expansion of contractor-owned facilities or acquisition of fixed assets.

Contract Financing Methods
- Advance payments—advances of money by the government to a prime contractor;

- Progress payments based on costs—made on the basis of costs incurred by the contract or as work progresses;

- Loan guarantees—guarantees backed by the Federal Reserve designed to enable contractors to obtain financing from private sources;

- Partial payments for accepted supplies and services—more of a payment versus financing method;

- Progress payments based on a percentage or stage of completion—again, more of a payment versus financing method;

- Performance-based payments—made on the basis of performance measured by objective, quantifiable methods, accomplishment of defined events, or other quantifiable measures of results.

Order of Preference

Private financing without government guarantee (it is not intended, however, that the contractor be required to obtain private financing at unreasonable terms or from other agencies), customary contract financing, loan guarantees, unusual contract financing, advance payments.

Unusual contract financing is any contract financing arrangement that deviates from customary contract financing procedures delineated in FAR Part 32.113. Offerors may propose only the customary contract financing specified in the solicitation.

If the contractor is a small business concern, the contracting officer must give special attention to meeting the contractor's financial need. A contractor's receipt of a Certificate of Competency from the Small Business Administration has no bearing on the contractor's need for or entitlement to contract financing.

B. Commercial Item Purchase Financing (FAR 32.2)

For purchases of commercial items, financing of the contract is normally the contractor's responsibility. However, in some markets, the provision of financing by the buyer is a commercial practice. In these circumstances, the contracting officer may include appropriate financing terms in contracts for commercial purchases when doing so will be in the best interest of the government.

Commercial interim payments and commercial advance payments may be made under the following circumstances: contract item financed is a commercial supply or service; contract price exceeds simplified acquisition threshold; contracting officer determines it is appropriate/customary in the commercial marketplace to make financing payments for the item and determines it is in the best interest of the government; adequate security is obtained; or aggregate of commercial advance payments shall not exceed 15 percent of contract price (competitive environment). If contract is sole source, adequate consideration obtained; and concurrence from the payment office regarding liquidation provisions, if required.

Types of Payments for Commercial Item Purchases

Commercial Advance Payment: payment made before any performance of work under the contract; aggregate payments shall not exceed 15 percent of the contract price; payments are not subject to FAR 32.4, Advance Payments for Non-Commercial Items.

Commercial Interim Payment: payment that is not a commercial advance payment or a delivery payment; interim payment is given to the contractor after some work has been done.

Delivery Payment: payment for accepted supplies or services, including payments for accepted partial deliveries.

Contract financing can be a subject included in the market research conducted in accordance with FAR Part 10 to determine the extent to which other buyers provide contract financing, the level of financing normally provided, the basis for and frequency of any payments, and methods of liquidation of contract financing payments, as well as any special or unusual payment terms applicable to delivery payments.

The contracting officer must calculate the time value of proposal-specified contract financing arrangements using the nominal discount rate specified in Appendix C of the Office of Management and Budget (OMB) Circular A-94, "Guidelines and Discount Rates for Benefit-Cost Analysis of Federal Programs" as the interest rate.

C. Loan Guarantees for Defense Production (FAR 32.3)

Federal Reserve Banks are authorized to act, on behalf of guaranteeing agencies (e.g., DOD), as fiscal agents of the United States in the making of loan guarantees for defense production. Guaranteed loans are essentially the same as conventional loans made by private financial institutions, except that the guaranteeing agency is obligated, on demand of the lender, to purchase a stated percentage of the loan and to share any losses in the amount of guaranteed percentage.

D. Advance Payments for Non-Commercial Items (FAR 32.4)

The least preferred method of contract financing should not be authorized if other types of financing are reasonably available to the contractor. Applicability limited to contracts described in FAR 32.403.

E. Progress Payments Based on Costs (FAR 32.5)

Customary progress payment rate is 80 percent for large business concerns and 85 percent for small business concerns. Any percentage greater than these is considered unusual.

Unusual progress payments may be applied only when the contract necessitates predelivery expenditures that are large in relation to contract price and in relation to the contractor's working capital and credit, the contractor fully documents an actual need to supplement any private financing available, and the contractor's request is approved by the head of the contracting activity.

Progress payments may be reduced or suspended when certain conditions exist.

Progress payments are recouped by the government through the deduction of liquidations from payments that would otherwise be due to the contractor for completed contract items.

The contracting officer must reject as nonresponsive those bids conditioned on progress payments when the solicitation did not provide for progress payments.

F. Contract Funding (FAR 32.7)

No officer or employee of the government may create or authorize an obligation in excess of the funds available, or in advance of appropriations unless otherwise authorized by law (Anti-Deficiency Act).

Before executing a contract, the contracting officer must obtain written assurance from responsible fiscal authority that adequate funds are available or expressly condition the contract upon availability of funds.

Contract action in support of operational and maintenance and continuing services requirements properly chargeable to funds of a new fiscal year may be initiated before these funds are available, provided that the contract includes the prescribed Availability of Funds clause.

A contract funded by annual appropriations may not generally cross fiscal years; however, indefinite-quantity or requirements contracts for services that are funded by annual appropriations may extend beyond the fiscal year in which they begin, provided that any specified minimum quantities are ordered in the initial fiscal year and the contract includes the prescribed Availability of Funds for the Next Fiscal Year clause.

Supplies or services under a contract conditioned upon the availability of funds cannot be accepted until after the contracting officer has given the contractor notice that funds are available.

Contracts that contain a Limitation of Cost or Funds clause must also be monitored closely. The contracting officer, upon learning that the contractor is approaching the estimated cost or limit of funds allotted must promptly notify the contractor in writing that (1) additional funds have been allotted or the estimated cost increased, (2) the contract will not be further funded, (3) the contract is to be terminated, or (4) the government is considering whether to allot additional funds or increase the estimated cost.

G. Assignment of Claims (FAR 32.8)

Assignment of Claims means the transfer or making over by the contractor to a bank, trust company, or other financing institution, as security for a loan to the contractor, of its right to be paid by the government for contract performance.

A contractor may assign monies due or to become due under a government order/contract only when its value exceeds $1,000; the assignment is made to a bank, trust company, or other financing institution; the contractual document does not prohibit the assignment; and the assignee sends a written notice of the assignment to the contracting officer or the agency head.

H. Prompt Payment (FAR 32.9)

Solicitations and contracts must specify payment procedures, payment due dates, and interest penalties for late invoice payment. Payments are generally made on the 30th day after the designated billing office receives a proper invoice from the contractor or the 30th day after government acceptance of supplies delivered or services performed by the contractor, whichever is later. Payment will be based on receipt of a proper invoice and satisfactory contract performance.

Discounts for prompt payment may be taken only when payments are made within the discount period specified by the contractor.

Agencies must pay interest for late invoice payments or improperly taken discounts for prompt payment.

I. Performance-Based Payments (FAR 32.10)

Performance-based payments are the preferred financing method when the contracting officer finds them practical, and the contractor agrees to their use. Performance-based payments are contract financing payments that are not payment for accepted items. Performance-based payments are fully recoverable, in the same manner as progress payments, in the event of default.

Conditions for Use
The contracting officer may use performance-based payments only if the following conditions are met:

- The contracting officer and offeror are able to agree on the performance-based payment terms;

- The contract is a fixed-price type contract;

- For indefinite-delivery contracts, the individual order does not provide for progress payments; and

- For other than indefinite-delivery contracts, the contract does not provide for progress payments.

The basis for performance-based payments may be either specifically described events (e.g., milestones) or some measurable criterion of performance. Note, however, that the signing of contracts or modifications, the exercise of options, or other such actions may *not* form the basis for such payments.

J. Electronic Funds Transfer (FAR 32.11)

Electronic funds transfer (EFT) means any transfer of funds, other than a transaction originated by cash, check, or similar paper instrument, that is initiated through an electronic terminal, telephone, computer, or magnetic tape, or the purpose of ordering, instructing, or authorizing a financial institution to debit or credit an account.

The government shall provide all contract payments through EFT, except the provisions found at FAR 32.1103 (a)-(i).

FAR Part 33. Protests, Disputes, and Appeals

A. Protests (FAR 33.1)

A protest is a written objection by an interested party to any of the following: a solicitation or other request by an agency for offers; cancellation of a solicitation or other request; an award or proposed award of a contract; or a termination or cancellation of an award of a contract as long as the written objection contains an allegation that the termination or cancellation is based in whole or in part on improprieties concerning the award of the contract. It may be filed with either the agency or the Government Accountability Office (GAO). See FAR Part 19 for protests of small business status, disadvantaged business status, HUB-Zone small business status, service-disabled veteran-owned small business status, EDWOSB, and WOSB.

Contracting officers shall consider all protests and seek legal advice, whether protests are submitted before or after award and whether filed directly with the agency or the GAO. Upon receipt of a protest before award, the affected contract may not be awarded pending agency resolution of the protest, unless continued performance is properly justified (urgent and compelling or best interest of the government).

With respect to any protest filed with the GAO, if the funds available to the agency for a contract at the time a protest is filed in connection with a solicitation for, proposed award of, or award of such a contract would otherwise expire, such funds remain available for obligation for 100 days after the date on which the final ruling is rendered.

Protests based on alleged apparent improprieties in a solicitation shall be filed before bid opening or the closing date for receipt of proposals. In all other cases, protests shall be filed no later than 10 days after the basis of protest is known or should have been known, whichever is earlier. The agency, for good cause shown, or where it determines that a protest raises issues significant to the agency's acquisition system, may consider the merits of any protest which is not timely filed.

General Procedures: Within one work day of filing a protest with GAO, a copy must be provided the contracting officer. He or she must immediately give notice of the protest to the contractor if the award has been made, or if no award has been made, to all parties who appear to have a reasonable prospect of receiving award if the protest is denied. Within 30 days (20 if express option is used) after notification, the contracting officer must submit a complete report (see FAR 33.104(a)(3)(i) for contents) to the GAO, with a copy to the protester and any other interested parties. The protester and other interested parties are required to furnish a copy of any comments on the agency report directly to the GAO within 10 days (five if express option is used) after receipt, with copies to the contracting officer and to other participating interested parties. If a hearing is held, these comments are due within five days thereafter.

Protests before award: Upon notification from the GAO of a protest, the contracting officer is barred from awarding subject contract unless authorized by the head of the contracting activity in writing and even then only after GAO is so notified.

Protests after award: If notified within 10 calendar days after award, or within five days after a debriefing date offered to the protester for any debriefing that is required by 15.505 or 15.506, whichever is later, the contracting officer must immediately suspend performance or terminate the awarded contract unless authorized by the head of the contracting activity in writing and even then, performance cannot resume until after GAO has been so notified. When the contracting officer receives notice of a protest filed with the GAO more than 10 calendar days after award, or five days after the debriefing, whichever is later, the contracting officer need not suspend contract performance or terminate the awarded contract unless he or she believes that an award may be invalidated and a delay in receiving the supplies or services is not prejudicial to the government's interest.

B. Disputes and Appeals (FAR 33.2)

A claim is a written demand or written assertion by one of the contracting parties seeking, as a matter of right, the payment of money in a sum certain, the adjustment or interpretation of contract terms, or other relief arising under or relating to the contract. However, a written demand or written assertion by the contractor seeking the payment of money exceeding $100,000 is not a claim under the Contracts Disputes Act of 1978 until certified as required by the Act and FAR 33.207.

The Contract Disputes Act of 1978, as amended, establishes procedures and requirements for asserting and resolving claims subject to the act. It also provides for the payment of interest on contractor claims, certification of contractor claims, and a civil penalty for contractor claims that are fraudulent or based on misrepresentation of fact.

It is the government's policy to try to resolve all contractual issues in controversy by mutual agreement at the contracting officer's level.

Claims in excess of $100,000, or regardless of the amount claimed when using arbitration pursuant to 5 U.S.C. 575-580 or any other alternate dispute resolution (ADR) technique, must be accompanied by a certification that states the claim is made in good faith, supporting data are accurate and complete to the best of the contractor's knowledge and belief, and the amount requested accurately reflects the contract adjustment for which the contractor believes the government is liable. The aggregate amount of both increased and decreased costs shall be used to determine whether or not the claim meets the dollar threshold requiring certification.

When a claim by or against a contractor cannot be satisfied or settled by mutual agreement and a decision on the claim is necessary, the matter is resolved through issuance of a contracting officer's final decision. The contracting officer shall issue the decision within the following statutory time limits: for claims of $100,000 or less—60 days after receiving a written request from the contractor that a decision be rendered within that period, or within a reasonable time after receipt of a claim if the contractor does not make such a request; for claims over $100,000—60 days after receipt of certification; provided, however, that if a decision will not be issued within 60 days, the contracting officer notifies the contractor, within that period, of the time within which a decision will be issued. Failure of the contracting officer to render a final decision within the required time period is deemed to constitute denial of the claim thereby authorizing the contractor to file an appeal or suit on the claim.

Alternative dispute resolution (ADR) refers to any procedure or combination of procedures voluntarily used to resolve issues in controversy. These procedures include, but are not limited to, conciliation, facilitation, mediation, fact-finding, mini trials, arbitration, and use of ombudsmen.

Issue in controversy means a material disagreement between the government and the contractor that may result in a claim or is a part of an existing claim.

The objective of using ADR procedures is to increase the opportunity for relatively inexpensive and expeditious resolution of issues in controversy. Essential elements thereof are existence of an issue in controversy, a voluntary election by both parties to participate in the ADR process, agreement on alternative procedures and terms to be used in lieu of formal litigation, participation in the process by officials of both parties who have the authority to resolve the issue in controversy, and contractor certification on any claim exceeding $100,000. ADR procedures may be used at any time that the contracting officer has authority to resolve the issue in controversy.

FAR Part 34. Major Systems Acquisition

This part describes acquisition policies and procedures used to contract for major systems and the use of an earned value management system. This part also references OMB Circulars for further guidance.

These policies are designed to ensure that agencies acquire major systems in the most effective, economical, and timely manner. They are intended to promote innovation and full and open competition as well as sustain effective competition between alternative system concepts and sources for as long as it is beneficial. The program manager shall develop an acquisition strategy tailored to the particular major system acquisition program.

Major systems are directed at and critical to fulfilling an agency mission need, will require allocating a large amount of resources, and warrant special management attention, including specific agency-head decisions.

Solicitations should be mission oriented and describe the nature of the need in terms of mission capabilities and refrain from specific reference to systems. It should also require the use of an earned value management system.

Through this process different types of contracts may be awarded as appropriate and consistent with agency budgets and mission. These contracts include concept exploration contracts, demonstration contracts, and full-scale development contracts, all of which would hopefully culminate in a contract for full Production

A. Testing, Qualification, and Use of Industrial Resources Developed Under Title III, Defense Production Act (FAR 34.1)

It is the policy of the government to pay for any testing and qualification required for the use or incorporation of the industrial resources manufactured or developed with assistance provided under Title III of the Defense Production Act of 1950. Contractors receiving requests from a Title III project contractor for testing and qualification of a Title III industrial resource shall refer such requests to the contracting officer.

B. Earned Value Management System (FAR 34.2)

An earned value management system (EVMS) is a project management tool that compares cost and schedule performance to predict future performance trends and determine whether objectives can be achieved with the proposed solution, schedule, and budget.

When an EVMS is required, the government will conduct an integrated baseline review (IBR) to verify the technical content and the realism of the related performance budgets, resources, and schedules. It should provide a mutual understanding of the inherent risks in offerors'/contractors' performance plans and the underlying management control systems, and it should formulate a plan to handle these risks.

The IBR is a joint assessment by the offeror or contractor, and the government, of the ability of the project's technical plan to achieve the objectives of the scope of work; the adequacy of the time allocated for performing the defined tasks to successfully achieve the project schedule objectives; the ability of the performance measurement baseline (PMB) to successfully execute the project and attain cost objectives, recognizing the relationship between budget resources, funding, schedule, and scope of work. It should also identify the availability of personnel, facilities, and equipment when required, as well as the degree to which the management process provides effective and integrated technical/schedule/cost planning and baseline control.

FAR Part 35. Research and Development Contracting

The primary purpose of contracted research and development (R&D) programs is to advance scientific and technical knowledge and apply that knowledge to the extent necessary to achieve agency and national goals. Unlike contracts for supplies and services, most R&D contracts are directed toward objectives for which the work or methods cannot be precisely described in advance. R&D solicitations shall require offerors to describe their technical and management approach, identify technical uncertainties, and make specific proposals for the resolution of any uncertainties. Selecting the appropriate contract type is the responsibility of the contracting officer. However, because of the importance of technical considerations in R&D, the choice of contract type should be made after obtaining the recommendations of technical personnel. The contracting process shall be used to encourage the best sources from the scientific and industrial community to become involved in the program and must provide an environ-

ment in which the work can be pursued with reasonable flexibility and minimum administrative burden.

In reviewing work statements, contracting officers should ensure that language suitable for a level-of-effort approach, which requires the furnishing of technical effort and a report on the results, is not intermingled with language suitable for a task-completion approach, which often requires the development of a tangible end item designed to achieve specific performance characteristics. The wording of the work statement should also be consistent with the type and form of contract to be negotiated. For example, the work statement for a cost-reimbursement contract promising the contractor's best efforts for a fixed term would be phrased differently than a work statement for a cost-reimbursement completion contract promising the contractor's best efforts for a defined task. Differences between work statements for fixed-price contracts and cost-reimbursement contracts should be even clearer.

FAR Part 36. Construction and Architect-Engineer Contracts

Construction and architect-engineer contracts are subject to the requirements in other parts of the *FAR*, which shall be followed when applicable. When a requirement in this part is inconsistent with a requirement in another part of this regulation, Part 36 shall take precedence if the acquisition of construction or architect-engineer services is involved. A contract for both construction and supplies or services shall include clauses applicable to the predominant part of the work or, if the contract is divided into parts, the clauses applicable to each portion.

A. Methods of Contracting (FAR 36.1)

Contracting officers shall acquire construction using sealed bid procedures for construction contracts performed in the United States.

Contracting officers shall acquire architect-engineer services by negotiation.

B. Special Aspects of Contacting for Construction (FAR 36.2)

An independent government estimate of construction costs shall be prepared and furnished to the contracting officer for each proposed contract and contract modification anticipated to exceed the simplified acquisition threshold. Advance notices and solicitations shall state the magnitude of the requirement in terms of physical characteristics and estimated price range. In no event shall the statement of magnitude disclose the government's estimate. In general, no contract for the construction of a project shall be awarded to the firm that designed the project or its subsidiaries or affiliates. Also, it is generally prohibited to have cost-reimbursement contracts operating concurrently with fixed price contracts on the same site. Agencies are required to implement high-performance sustainable building principles for design, construction, renovation, repair, commissioning, operation and maintenance, management, and demolition of federal buildings.

FAR Part 37. Service Contracting

This part prescribes policy and procedures that are specific to the acquisition and management of services by contract. This part applies to all contracts and orders for services regardless of the contract type or kind of service being acquired. This part requires the use of performance-based acquisitions for services to the maximum extent practicable and prescribes policies and procedures for use of performance-based acquisition methods.

A. Service Contracts—General (FAR 37.1)

A *Nonpersonal services contract* is a contract under which the personnel rendering the services are not subject, either by the contract's terms or by the manner of its administration, to the supervision and control usually prevailing in relationships between the government and its employees.

A *service contract* means a contract that directly engages the time and effort of a contractor whose primary purpose is to perform an identifiable task rather than to furnish an end item of supply. A service contract may be either a nonpersonal or personal contract.

Agencies shall generally rely on the private sector for commercial services. Agencies shall not award a contract for the performance of an inherently governmental function.

A personal services contract is characterized by the employer–employee relationship it creates between the government and the contractor's personnel. The government is normally required to obtain its employees by direct hire under competitive appointment or other procedures required by the civil service laws. Obtaining personal services by contract, rather than by direct hire, circumvents those laws unless Congress has specifically authorized acquisition of the services by contract.

An employer–employee relationship under a service contract occurs when, as a result of either the contract's terms or the manner of its administration during performance, contractor personnel are subject to the relatively continuous supervision and control of a government officer or employee. Each contract arrangement must be judged in the light of its own facts and circumstances, the key question always being: Will the government exercise relatively continuous supervision and control over the contractor personnel performing the contract?

Giving an order for a specific article or service, with the right to reject the finished product or result, is not the type of supervision or control that converts an individual who is an independent contractor (such as a contractor employee) into a government employee. The sporadic, unauthorized supervision of only one of a large number of contractor employees might reasonably be considered not relevant, while relatively continuous government supervision of a substantial number of contractor employees would have to be taken strongly into account.

The following descriptive elements should be used as a guide in assessing whether a proposed contract is personal in nature:

- Performance on the government's site;

- Principal tools and equipment furnished by the government;

- Services are applied directly to the integral effort of agencies or an organizational subpart in furtherance of assigned function or mission;

- Comparable services, meeting comparable needs, are performed in the same or similar agencies using civil service personnel;

- The need for the type of service provided can reasonably be expected to last beyond one year; and

- The inherent nature of the service, or the manner in which it is provided, reasonably requires directly or indirectly, government direction or supervision of contractor employees in order to

  o Adequately protect the government's interest;

  o Retain control of the function involved; or

  o Retain full personal responsibility for the function supported in a duly authorized federal officer or employee.

The head of an executive agency, except NASA, may contract for severable services for a period that begins in one fiscal year and ends in the next fiscal year if the term does not exceed one year.

Award of contracts for recurring and continuing service requirements are often delayed due to circumstances beyond the control of contracting offices. Examples of circumstances causing such delays are bid protests and alleged mistakes in bid. In order to avoid negotiation of short extensions to existing contracts, the contracting officer may include an option clause (FAR 17.208(f)) in solicitations and contracts which will enable the government to require continued performance of any services within the limits and at the rates specified in the contract.

However, these rates may be adjusted only as a result of revisions to prevailing labor rates provided by the Secretary of Labor. The option provision may be exercised more than once, but the total extension of performance thereunder shall not exceed six months.

Contracting officers must ensure that the uncompensated overtime in contracts to acquire services on the basis of the number of hours provided will not degrade the level of technical expertise required to fulfill the government's requirements. When acquiring these services, contracting officers must conduct a risk assessment and evaluate, for award on that basis, any proposals received that reflect factors such as unrealistically low labor rates or unbalanced distribution of uncompensated overtime among skill levels and its use in key technical positions.

B. Advisory and Assistance Services (FAR 37.2)

The acquisition of advisory and assistance services is a legitimate way to improve government services and operations. Accordingly, advisory and assistance services may be used at all organizational levels to help managers achieve maximum effectiveness or economy in their operations. Examples of appropriate uses include obtaining outside points of view to avoid limited judgment on critical issues, obtaining advice regarding developments in industry, university, or foundation research, and obtaining the opinions, special knowledge, or skills of noted experts. It is also useful to enhance the understanding of and develop alternative solutions to complex issues. From a managerial perspective it can support and improve the operation of organizations or ensure more efficient or effective operation of managerial or hardware systems.

C. Dismantling, Demolition, or Removal of Improvements (FAR 37.3)

Contracts for dismantling, demolition, or removal of improvements are subject to either the Service Contract Act or the Davis-Bacon Act. If the contract is solely for dismantling, demolition, or removal of improvements, the Service Contract Act applies unless further work which will result in the construction, alteration, or repair of a public building or public work at that location is contemplated. If such further construction work is intended, even though by separate contract, then the Davis-Bacon Act applies to the contract for dismantling, demolition, or removal.

FAR Part 38. Federal Supply Schedule Contracting

The Federal Supply Schedule program provides federal agencies with a simplified process of acquiring commercial supplies and services in varying quantities while obtaining discounts associated with volume buying. Indefinite delivery contracts are awarded, using competitive procedures, to commercial firms to provide supplies and services at stated prices for given periods of time, for delivery within the 48 contiguous states; Washington, DC; and Alaska, Hawaii, and overseas deliveries.

Each schedule identifies agencies that are required to use the contracts as primary sources of supply. Federal agencies not identified in the schedules as mandatory users may issue orders under the schedules. Contractors are encouraged to accept the orders. Although GSA awards most Federal Supply Schedule contracts, it may authorize other agencies to award schedule contracts and publish schedules. For example, the Department of Veterans Affairs awards schedule contracts for certain medical and nonperishable subsistence items.

FAR Part 39. Acquisition of Information Technology

Modular contracting is the use of one or more contracts to acquire information technology systems in successive, interoperable increments.

National security system means any telecommunications or information system operated by the U.S. government; the function, operation, or use of which involves intelligence activities; cryptologic activities related to national defense, command, and control of military forces; equipment that is an integral part of a weapon system; or is critical to the direct fulfillment of military or intelligence missions.

Agencies shall insure that contracts for information technology address protection of privacy in accordance with the Privacy Act.

A. General (FAR 39.1)

Prior to entering into a contract for information technology, an agency should analyze risks, benefits, and costs. Reasonable risk-taking is appropriate as long as risks are controlled and mitigated. Types of risk may include schedule risk, risk of technical obsolescence, cost risk, risk implicit in a particular contract type, technical feasibility, dependencies between a new project and other projects or systems, the number of simultaneous high risk projects to be monitored, funding availability, and program management risk. Appropriate techniques should be applied to manage and mitigate risk during the acquisition of information technology.

Modular contracting is intended to reduce program risk and to incentivize contractor performance while meeting the government's need for timely access to rapidly changing technology. Consistent with the agency's information technology architecture, agencies should, to the maximum extent practicable, use modular contracting to acquire major systems of information technology.

The characteristics of an increment used in modular contracting may vary depending upon the type of information technology being acquired and the nature of the system being developed.

To promote compatibility, the information technology acquired through modular contracting for each increment should comply with common or commercially acceptable information technology standards when available and appropriate, and shall conform to the agency's master information technology architecture. Additionally the performance requirements of each increment should be consistent with the performance requirements of the completed, overall system within which the information technology will function and should address interface requirements with succeeding increments.

For each increment, contracting officers shall choose an appropriate contracting technique that facilitates the acquisition of subsequent increments. Contracts shall be structured to ensure that the government is not required to procure additional increments.

To avoid obsolescence, a modular contract for information technology should, be awarded within 180 days after the date on which the solicitation is issued. If award cannot be made within 180 days, agencies should consider

cancellation of the solicitation. To the maximum extent practicable, deliveries under the contract should be scheduled to occur within 18 months after issuance of the solicitation.

B. Electronic and Information Technology (FAR 39.2)

This subpart implements section 508 of the Rehabilitation Act of 1973. This ensures that both federal employees with disabilities and members of the public seeking service from the government have equal access to the technology as nondisabled members of the public and employees.

This requirement does not apply if the electronic and information technology (EIT) is a micro-purchase; is for a national security system; is acquired by a contractor incidental to a contract; is located in spaces frequented only by service personnel for maintenance, repair, or occasional monitoring of equipment; or would impose an undue burden on the agency.

Section
SIX
FAR Parts 42–51

Agencies shall avoid duplicate audits, reviews, inspections, and examinations of contractors or subcontractors, by more than one agency through the use of interagency agreements. Subject to the fiscal regulations of the agencies and applicable interagency agreements, the requesting agency shall reimburse the servicing agency for rendered services in accordance with the Economy Act (31 U.S.C. 1535). When an interagency agreement is established, the agencies are encouraged to consider establishing procedures for the resolution of issues that may arise under the agreement.

A. Contract Audit Services (FAR 42.1)

The auditor is responsible for submitting information and advice to the requesting activity, based on the auditor's analysis of the contractor's financial and accounting records or other related data as to the acceptability of the contractor's incurred and estimated costs; reviewing the financial and accounting aspects of the contractor's cost control systems; and performing other analyses and reviews that require access to the contractor's financial and accounting records supporting proposed and incurred costs.

B. Contract Administration Services (FAR 42.2)

This prescribes policies and procedures for assigning, retaining, or reassigning contract administration responsibility; withholding normal functions or delegating additional functions when assigning contracts for administration; and requesting and performing supporting contract administration.

Contracting officers must retain for administration any contract not requiring the performance of contract administration functions at or near contractor facilities, or for which retention by the contracting office is prescribed

99

by agency acquisition regulations. However, a contract administration office or a contracting office retaining contract administration may request supporting contract administration from the contract administration office cognizant of the contractor location where performance of specific contract administration functions is required.

C. Contract Administration Office Functions (FAR 42.3)

Unless otherwise agreed to, the Contract Administration Office (CAO) will perform the functions listed in FAR 42.302(a) in accordance with the *FAR*, the contract terms, and the applicable regulations of the servicing agency. CAOs may also perform the functions delineated in FAR 42.302(b) only when and to the extent specifically authorized by the contracting office. Contract administration functions not listed in FAR 42.302, or not otherwise delegated, remain the responsibility of the contracting office.

D. Post-award Orientation (FAR 42.5)

This is designed to achieve a clear and mutual understanding of all contract requirements and to identify/resolve potential problems. This is not meant to substitute for contractor's fully understanding work requirements at the time offers were submitted or to alter the final agreement.

The contracting officer shall take into consideration the nature and extent of pre-award survey and other discussions; type, value and complexity of the contract; complexity and acquisition history of product/service; requirements for spare parts and related equipment; urgency of delivery schedule and relationship of the product or service to critical programs; length of planned production cycle; extent of subcontracting; contractor's performance history and experience; contractor's status (small business, small disadvantaged business, women-owned small business, veteran-owned business, HUBZone, service-disabled veteran–owned small business); contractor's performance history with small business, small disadvantaged business, women-owned small business, veteran-owned business, HUBZone, and service-disabled veteran–owned small business subcontracting programs; safety; and complexity of financial arrangements in the determination to hold a post-award conference. Post-award letters may be used in lieu of a conference where deemed appropriate by the contracting officer.

E. Corporate Administrative Contracting Officer (FAR 42.6)

Contractors with more than one operating location often have corporate-wide policies and procedures requiring government review and approval. For consistency, this is provided by the Corporate Administrative Contracting Officer (CACO).

A decision to initiate or discontinue a CACO should be based on the benefits of coordination and liaison at the corporate level; volume of government sales; degree of control the corporate office exercises over government sales divisions; and the impact of corporate policies and procedures on those divisions.

Responsibilities typically assigned to a CACO are determination of final indirect cost rates for cost reimbursement contracts; establishing advance agreements on corporate/home office expense allocations; and administration of CAS applicable to the corporate level.

F. Indirect Cost Rates (FAR 42.7)

Billing rate means an indirect cost rate established temporarily for interim reimbursement of incurred indirect costs and adjusted as necessary pending establishment of final indirect cost rates.

Billing rates and final indirect cost rates are used in reimbursing indirect costs under cost-reimbursement contracts and in determining progress payments under fixed-price contracts.

G. Disallowance of Costs (FAR 42.8)

At any time during the course of performance of a cost reimbursement, fixed-price incentive, or fixed-price with price redetermination contract, the ACO may issue a notice of intent to disallow specified costs incurred or planned for. In the event of disagreement, the contractor may submit a written response. The ACO must then answer or withdraw the notice within 60 days.

A notice of intent to disallow costs usually results from monitoring contractor costs. The purpose of the notice is to notify the contractor as early as practicable during contract performance that the cost is considered unallowable under the contract terms and to provide for timely resolution of any resulting disagreement.

H. Bankruptcy (FAR 42.9)

The contractor must notify the government immediately upon filing for bankruptcy. The contract administration office shall take prompt action to determine the potential impact of a contractor bankruptcy on the government in order to protect its interests.

Agencies shall, as a minimum, furnish the notice of bankruptcy to legal counsel and other appropriate agency offices (e.g., contracting, financial, property) and affected buying activities; determine the amount of the government's potential claim against the contractor (in assessing this impact, identify and review any contracts that have not been closed out, including those physically completed or terminated); take actions necessary to protect the government's financial interests and safeguard government property; and furnish pertinent contract information to the legal counsel representing the government.

The contracting officer shall consult with legal counsel, whenever possible, prior to taking any action regarding the contractor's bankruptcy proceedings.

I. Production Surveillance and Reporting (FAR 42.11)

Production surveillance is used to determine contractor progress and identify any factors that may cause delay. It involves government review and analysis of contractor performance plans, schedules, controls, and industrial processes relative to the contractor's actual performance.

Extent of surveillance is determined by assessing the criticality of supplies/services, contract reporting requirements, contract performance schedule, contractor's production plan, history of contract performance, experience with the supplies/services, and/or financial capacity. Surveillance should be tailored to the risk involved.

J. Novation and Change-of-Name Agreements (FAR 42.12)

A novation agreement recognizes a successor in interest to government contracts when the contractor's assets are transferred. A change-of-name agreement recognizes a legal change in the contractor's name. Both of these are affected through execution of a modification to the applicable contract(s).

K. Suspension of Work, Stop-Work Orders, and Government Delay of Work (FAR 42.13)

Suspension of Work may be ordered by the contracting officer for a reasonable period of time; applicable to construction or architectural and engineering contracts.

Stop-work orders are generally issued only if it is advisable to suspend work pending a decision by the government and a supplemental agreement is not feasible; applicable to any negotiated fixed-price or cost-reimbursement supply, research, development, or service contract.

Government delay of work does not authorize the contracting officer to order a suspension, delay, or interruption of work; and it is not to be used as the basis or justification of such an order.

L. Contractor Performance Information (FAR 42.15)

Past performance information is relevant information, for future source selection purposes, regarding a contractor's actions under previously awarded contracts. It includes, for example, the contractor's record of conforming to contract requirements and to standards of good workmanship; the contractor's record of forecasting and controlling costs; the contractor's adherence to contract schedules, including the administrative aspects of performance; the contractor's history of reasonable and cooperative behavior and commitment to customer satisfaction; the contractor's record of integrity and business ethics; and generally, the contractor's business-like concern for the interest of the customer.

Past performance evaluations shall be prepared at the time the work under the contract or order is completed. The content of the evaluations should be tailored to the size, content, and complexity of the contractual requirements. Past performance evaluations shall be prepared for each construction contract of $650,000 or more and for each architect-engineer services contract of $30,000 or more. Past performance evaluations are required for all other contracts greater than the Simplified Acquisition Threshold.

The ultimate conclusion on the performance evaluation is a decision of the contracting agency.

Agencies shall submit past performance reports electronically to the Past Performance Information Retrieval System (PPIRS). Agencies shall use the past performance information in PPIRS that is within three years (six for construction and architect-engineer contracts) of the completion of performance of the evaluated contract or order, and information contained in the Federal Awardee Performance and Integrity Information System (FAPIIS) (e.g., terminations for default or cause).

Agencies shall also submit past performance information in FAPIIS within three working days after a contracting officer

- Issues a final determination that a contractor has submitted defective cost or pricing data,

- Makes a subsequent change to the final determination concerning defective cost or pricing data,

- Issues a final termination for cause or default notice, or

- Makes a subsequent withdrawal or a conversion of a termination for default to a termination for convenience.

M. Small Business Contract Administration (FAR 42.16)

Contracting officers shall make every reasonable effort to respond to written requests from a small business concern within 30 days on matters of a contract administration nature.

N. Forward Pricing Rate Agreements (FAR 42.17)

Negotiation of forward pricing rate agreements (FPRAs) may be requested by the contracting officer or the contractor or initiated by the administrative contracting officer (ACO). In determining whether to establish an FPRA, the ACO should consider whether the benefits to be derived from the agreement are commensurate with the effort of establishing and monitoring it. Normally, FPRAs should be negotiated only with contractors having a significant volume of government contract proposals.

The FPRA shall provide specific terms and conditions covering expiration, application, and data requirements for systematic monitoring to ensure the validity of the rates. The agreement shall provide for cancellation at the option of either party and shall require the contractor to submit to the ACO and to the cognizant contract auditor any significant change in cost or pricing data used to support the FPRA.

FAR Part 43. Contract Modifications

A. General Policy (FAR 43.1)

Only contracting officers acting within the scope of their authority are empowered to execute contract modifications on behalf of the government. Other government personnel shall not execute contract modifications, act in such a manner as to cause the contractor to believe that they have authority to bind the government, or direct or encourage the contractor to perform work that should be the subject of a contract modification.

Contract modifications can be either

- Bilateral (supplemental agreement)—to make negotiated equitable adjustments resulting from a change order, definitize letter contracts, and reflect other agreements modifying the terms and conditions; or

- Unilateral—to make administrative changes, issue change orders, make changes authorized by clauses other than the changes clause, as well as issue termination notices.

Modifications that cause or will cause an increase in funds are not to be executed absent certification of funds availability.

Contract modifications have different effective dates depending upon the type of modification. For a solicitation amendment, change order, or administrative change, the effective date shall be the issue date of the amendment, change order, or administrative change. For a supplemental agreement, the effective date shall be the date agreed upon by the contracting parties. For a modification issued as a confirming notice of termination for the convenience of the government, the effective date of the confirming notice shall be the same as the effective date of the initial notice. For a modification converting a termination for default to a termination for the convenience of the government, the effective date shall be the same as the effective date of the termination for default. For a modification confirming the termination, the contracting officer's previous letter determination of the amount due in settlement of a contract termination for convenience, the effective date shall be the same as the effective date of the previous letter determination.

B. Change Orders (FAR 43.2)

Generally, government contracts contain a changes clause permitting the contracting officer to make unilateral changes in designated areas within the scope of the contract.

Upon receipt of a change order, the contractor may not cease work but must rather comply with the change (i.e., the contractor has an obligation to proceed), except that in cost-reimbursement or incrementally funded contracts the contractor is not obligated beyond the limits of the Limitation of Cost clause or Funds clause. If the contractor's request for equitable adjustment is denied by the contracting officer, then the contractor may consider initiating a claim. (FAR 33.206)

When change orders are not forward priced, they require two documents: the change order and a supplemental agreement reflecting the resulting equitable adjustment in contract terms. Negotiation of equitable adjustments resulting from change orders should be effected in the shortest practicable time.

A. Consent to Subcontract (FAR 44.2)

If the contractor has an approved purchasing system, consent is required for subcontracts specifically identified by the contracting officer in the subcontracts clause of the contract. If the contractor does not have an approved purchasing system, consent to subcontract is required for cost-reimbursement, time-and-materials, labor-hour, or letter contracts, and also for unpriced actions under fixed-price contracts that exceed the simplified acquisition threshold for cost-reimbursement, time-and-materials, or labor-hour subcontracts and fixed-price subcontracts.

The contracting officer's written authorization for the contractor to purchase from government sources constitutes consent.

B. Contractor Purchasing Systems Reviews (FAR 44.3)

The objective of a contractor purchasing system review (CSPR) is to evaluate the efficiency and effectiveness with which the contractor spends government funds and complies with government policy when subcontracting. The review provides the administrative contracting officer (ACO) a basis for granting, withholding, or withdrawing approval of the contractor's purchasing system

Contractor-acquired property is property acquired, fabricated, or otherwise provided by the contractor for performing a contract and to which the government has title.

Government-furnished property is property in the possession of, or directly acquired by, the government and subsequently furnished to the contractor for performance of a contract.

Government property is all property owned by or leased to the government or acquired by the government under the terms of the contract. It includes both government-furnished property and contractor-acquired property.

Agencies will not generally require contractors to establish property management systems that are separate from a contractor's established procedures, practices, and systems used to account for and manage contractor-owned property.

Generally, contractors are not held liable for loss of government property under the following types of contracts under cost-reimbursement, time-and-material, labor-hour, or fixed-price contracts awarded on the basis of certified cost or pricing data.

Contracts that include Alternate I to the standard FAR-52.245-1, Government Property, are the exception.

Government property shall normally be provided on a rent-free basis in performance of the contract under which it is accountable or otherwise authorized. The contracting officer cognizant of the government property may authorize the rent-free use of property in the possession of nonprofit organizations when used for research, development, or educational work and if it will not be used for the direct benefit of a profit-making organization and the government receives some benefit or it is in the national interest.

Requests by, or for the benefit of, foreign governments or international organizations to use government property shall be processed in accordance with agency procedures.

A. General (FAR 46.1)

Acceptance means the act of an authorized representative of the government by which the government, for itself or as agent of another, assumes ownership of existing identified supplies tendered or approves specific services rendered as partial or complete performance of the contract.

Latent defect means a defect that exists at the time of acceptance but cannot be discovered by a reasonable inspection.

Patent defect means any defect that exists at the time of acceptance and is not a latent defect.

B. Contract Quality Requirements (FAR 46.2)

Contract quality requirements fall into four general categories, depending on the extent of quality assurance needed by the government for the acquisition involved:

1. When acquiring commercial items, the government shall rely on contractors' existing quality assurance systems;

2. For most acquisitions at or below the simplified acquisition threshold, the government shall rely on the contractor to accomplish all inspection and testing;

3. Standard inspection requirements; or

4. Higher-level contract quality requirements for complex or critical items. Examples of higher-level quality standards are ISO 9001, 9002, or 9003; ANSI/ASQC9001, Q9002, or Q9003; QS9000; AS-9000; ANSI/ASQC E4; and ANSI/ASME NQA-1.

C. Government Contract Quality Assurance (FAR 46.4)

Government contract quality assurance shall be performed at such times and places as may be necessary to determine that the supplies or services conform to contract requirements. Quality assurance surveillance plans should be prepared in conjunction with the preparation of the statement of work. The plans should specify all work requiring surveillance and the method of surveillance.

Government quality assurance can be performed at either the source or destination, whichever is most appropriate.

When supplies or services are accepted with critical or major nonconformances as authorized by the *FAR*, the contracting officer must modify the contract to provide for an equitable price reduction or other consideration. If the nonconformance is minor, the cognizant contract administration office may make the determination to accept or reject, except where this authority is withheld by the contracting office of the contracting activity.

D. Acceptance (FAR 46.5)

Acceptance constitutes acknowledgment that the supplies or services conform with applicable contract quality and quantity requirements. Acceptance may take place before delivery, at the time of delivery, or after delivery, depending on the provisions of the terms and conditions of the contract. Supplies or services shall ordinarily not be accepted before completion of government contract quality assurance actions. Acceptance shall ordinarily be evidenced by execution of an acceptance certificate on an inspection or receiving report form or commercial shipping document/ packing list.

Acceptance of supplies or services is generally the responsibility of the contracting officer.

E. Warranties (FAR 46.7)

The principal purposes of a warranty in a government contract are to delineate the rights and obligations of the contractor and the government for defective items and services; and to foster quality performance. Generally, a warranty should provide a contractual right for the correction of defects notwithstanding any other requirement of the contract pertaining to acceptance of the supplies or services by the government and a stated period of time or use, or the occurrence of a specified event, after acceptance by the government to assert a contractual right for the correction of defects.

The benefits to be derived from a warranty must be commensurate with the cost of the warranty to the government. The use of a warranty is not mandatory.

Except for the warranties in the clauses at FAR 52.246-3, Inspection of Supplies—Cost Reimbursement, and FAR 52.246-8, Inspection of Research and Development—Cost Reimbursement, the contracting officer shall not include warranties in cost-reimbursement contracts. Additionally, warranty clauses shall not limit the government's rights under an inspection clause in relation to latent defects, fraud, or gross mistakes that amount to fraud. Except for warranty clauses in construction contracts, warranty clauses shall provide that the warranty applies notwithstanding inspection and acceptance or other clauses or terms of the contract.

FAR Part 47. Transportation

Applicability: applies to all government personnel concerned with the acquisition of supplies, acquisition of transportation and transportation-related services, transportation assistance and traffic management, administration of transportation contracts, transportation-related services, and other contracts that involve transportation, and the making and administration of contracts, under which payments are made from government funds.

Bill of lading means a transportation document, used as a receipt of goods, as documentary evidence of title, for clearing customs, and generally used as a contract of carriage.

- *Commercial bill of lading* (CBL), unlike the government bill of lading, is not an accountable transportation document.

- *Government bill of lading* (GBL) is an accountable transportation document, authorized and prepared by a government official.

- *Common carrier* means a person holding oneself out to the general public to provide transportation for compensation.

- *Contract carrier* means a person providing transportation for compensation under continuing agreement with one person or a limited number of persons.

F.O.B. (free on board) is a term used in conjunction with a physical point to determine the responsibility and basis for payment of freight charges; and unless otherwise agreed, the point at which title for goods passes to the buyer or consignee.

FAR Part 48. Value Engineering

Value engineering is the formal technique by which contractors may (1) voluntarily suggest methods for performing more economically and share in any resulting savings, or (2) be required to establish a program to identify and submit to the government methods for performing more economically.

There are two value engineering approaches: (1) An incentive approach in which contractor participation is voluntary and the contractor uses its own resources to develop and submit value engineering change proposals (VECPs). The contract provides for sharing of saving and for payment of the contractor's allowable development and implementation costs only if a VECP is approved. (2) A mandatory program in which the government requires and pays for a specific value engineering program effort.

As required by Section 36 of the Office of Federal Procurement Policy Act (41 U.S.C. 401, et seq.), agencies shall establish and maintain cost-effective value engineering procedures and processes. Agencies shall provide contractors a substantial financial incentive to develop and submit VECP's. Contracting activities will include value engineering provisions in appropriate supply, service, architect-engineer and construction contracts as prescribed by 48.201 and 48.202 except where exemptions are granted on a case-by-case basis, or for specific classes of contracts, by the agency head.

Agencies shall establish guidelines and process VECP's objectively and expeditiously providing contractors a fair share of the savings on accepted VECP's. Value engineering incentive payments do not constitute profit or fee, and generally profit or fee on the instant contract should not be adjusted downward. Profit or fee shall be excluded when calculating instant or future cost savings.

There are several mechanisms for calculating and sharing savings between the government and contractor, and the *FAR* must be carefully consulted to determine the approach most appropriate for the individual situation.

The following government decisions are unilateral decisions made solely at the discretion of the government:

- The decision to accept or reject a VECP;

- The determination of collateral costs or collateral savings;

- The decision as to which of the sharing rates applies when Alternate II of the clause at 52.248-1, Value Engineering, is used; and

- The contracting officer's determination of the duration of the sharing period and the contractor's sharing rate.

Generally, acquisition savings may be realized on the instant contract, concurrent contracts, and future contracts. The contractor is entitled to a percentage share of any net acquisition savings. Net acquisition savings result when the total of acquisition savings becomes greater than the total of government costs and any negative instant contract savings. This may occur until reductions have been negotiated on concurrent contracts or until future contract savings are calculated, either through lump-sum payment or as each future contract is awarded.

When the instant contract is not an incentive contract, the contractor's share of net acquisition savings is calculated and paid each time such savings are realized. This may occur once, several times, or in rare cases, not at all. When the instant contract is an incentive contract, the contractor shares in instant contract savings through the contract's incentive structure. In calculating acquisition savings under incentive contracts, the contracting officer shall add any negative instant contract savings to the target cost or to the target price and ceiling price and then offset these negative instant contract savings and any government costs against concurrent and future contract savings.

The government shares collateral savings with the contractor, unless the head of the contracting activity has determined that the cost of calculating and tracking collateral savings will exceed the benefits to be derived. The contractor's share of collateral savings may range from 20 to 100 percent of the estimated savings to be realized during a typical year of use but must not exceed the greater of the contract's firm-fixed-price, target price, target cost, or estimated cost, at the time the VECP is accepted or $100,000.

A. General Principles (FAR 49.1)

Termination for convenience or default is exercised by the government. No-cost settlements may be effected in lieu thereof only when it is known that the contractor will accept one, government-furnished property was not furnished, and there are no outstanding payments/debts due the government or other contractor obligations.

When the price of the undelivered balance of the contract is less than $5,000, the contract should not normally be terminated for convenience but rather permitted to reach completion.

If the same item is under contract with both a large and small business and it becomes necessary to terminate for convenience part of the units, preference will be given to continue performance of the small business over the large business unless not in the government's interest.

Terminations are generally settled by one of the following methods, in order of preference: negotiated agreement, terminating contracting officer (TCO) determination, costing out under SF 1034, or a combination of these methods.

After receiving notice of termination, the prime contractor shall stop work immediately on the terminated portion of the contract and stop placing subcontracts; terminate all subcontracts related to the terminated portion of the prime contract; immediately advise the TCO of any special circumstances precluding the stoppage of work; perform the continued portion of the contract and submit promptly any supported request for equitable adjustment; take necessary or directed action to protect and preserve government furnished property and deliver it to the government; promptly notify the TCO in writing of any

legal proceedings growing out of any subcontract or other commitment related to the terminated portion of the contract; settle outstanding liabilities; promptly submit the settlement proposal; and dispose of terminated inventory.

The TCO is responsible for directing the action required of the prime; examining, negotiating, and settling settlement proposals; sending the contracting officer periodic status reports; and estimating and recommending release of excess funds.

B. Additional Principles for Fixed-Price Contracts Terminated for Convenience (FAR 49.2)

A settlement should compensate the contractor fairly for the work done and the preparations made for the terminated portions of the contract, including a reasonable allowance for profit. The TCO shall allow profit on preparations made and work done by the contractor for the terminated portion of the contract but not on the settlement expenses. Anticipatory profits and consequential damages shall not be allowed. In the negotiation or determination of any settlement, the TCO shall not allow profit if it appears that the contractor would have incurred a loss had the entire contract been completed.

C. Termination for Default (FAR 49.4)

Termination for default is generally the exercise of the government's contractual right to completely or partially terminate a contract because of the contractor's actual or anticipated failure to perform its contractual obligations.

Under a termination for default, the government is not liable for the contractor's costs on undelivered work and is entitled to repayment of any advance and progress payments applicable to that work.

When a termination for default stems from failure to make delivery of supplies or perform services within the time specified in the contract, the contracting officer need only send a notice of termination. However, if it stems from the contractor's failure to perform some other provision of the contract or to make progress so as to endanger performance of the contract, the contracting officer must first issue a cure/show cause notice and allow the contractor at least 10 days to fix the problem.

In lieu of a termination for default, the TCO can consider permitting the contractor, surety, or guarantor to continue performance with a revised delivery schedule, allowing the contractor to continue through the use of subcontracts, or if the need for the supplies/services no longer exists, executing a no-cost settlement. If the surety does not arrange for completion of the contract, the contracting officer normally will arrange for completion of the work by awarding a new contract based on the same plans and specifications. The new contract may be the result of sealed bidding or any other appropriate contracting method or procedure. The contracting officer shall exercise reasonable diligence to obtain the lowest price available for completion.

FAR Part 49 does not apply to commercial item contracts awarded using Part 12 procedures; however, Part 49 provides administrative guidance which may be followed unless it is inconsistent with the requirements and procedures in FAR 12.403, Termination, and the clause at FAR 52.212-4, Contract Terms and Conditions—Commercial Items.

FAR Part 50. Extraordinary Contractual Actions

This part prescribes policies and procedures for entering into, or modifying contracts in order to facilitate the national defense under the extraordinary emergency authority granted by Public Law 85-804 (50 U.S.C. 1431—1434) and Executive Order 10789.

It does not cover advance payments. The act empowers the president to authorize agencies exercising function in connection with the national defense to enter into, amend, and modify contracts—without regard to other provisions of law related to making, performing, amending, or modifying contracts—whenever the president considers that such action would facilitate the national defense. Heads of the agencies listed at FAR 50.101(b) are authorized by executive order to exercise the authority conferred by the act and to delegate it to other officials within the agency.

FAR Part 51. Use of Government Sources by Contractors

A. Policy (FAR 51.101)

If it is in the government's interest, and if supplies or services required in the performance of a government contract are available from government supply sources, contracting officers may authorize contractors to use these sources in performing

- Government cost-reimbursement contracts;

- Other types of negotiated contracts when the agency determines that a substantial dollar portion of the contractor's contracts are of a government cost reimbursement nature; or

- A contract under the Javits-Wagner-O'Day Act, if;

  ○ The nonprofit agency requesting use of the supplies and services is providing a commodity or service to the federal government; and

  ○ The supplies or services received are directly used in making or providing a commodity or service, approved by the Committee for Purchase Ffrom People Who Are Blind or Severely Disabled, to the federal government.

B. Contract Clause (FAR 51.107)

The contracting officer shall insert the clause at 52.251-1, Government Supply Sources, in solicitations and contracts when the contracting officer may authorize the contractor to acquire supplies and services from a government supply source.

APPENDIX

CFCM Exam Practice Test

NOTE: There are two main purposes for this practice test—(1) to assist certification candidates in identifying areas of strengths and weaknesses and (2) to encourage candidates to familiarize themselves with parts of the *FAR* they do not consult on a regular basis.

Candidates should not assume that questions on the practice test are the same as those on the CFCM exam. Candidates should consult the NCMA website for the most current information concerning the number of actual exam questions drawn from each *FAR* part.)

FAR Part 1 (Contracting Authority and Responsibilities)

1. How often are statutory acquisition-related dollar thresholds in the *FAR* adjusted for inflation?

   a. annually
   b. bi-annually
   c. every five years
   d. only as required

   ANSWER: _____
   SOURCE(S): FAR 1.109

2. A form of written approval signed by an authorized official that is required by statute or regulation as a prerequisite to taking certain contract actions is defined as

   a. a ratification.
   b. Determination and Findings.
   c. the Contracting Officer's Final Decision.
   d. a waiver.

   ANSWER: _____
   SOURCE(S): FAR 1.701

3. Contracting officers below the level of _____ shall be selected and appointed.

   a. cabinet secretary
   b. director of contracting
   c. a flag officer or member of the Senior Executive Service
   d. a head of a contracting activity

ANSWER: _____
SOURCE(S): FAR 1.601

FAR Part 2 (Definitions of Words and Terms)

4. The simplified acquisition threshold for any contract in support of contingency operations to be awarded and performed, or purchase to be made, outside the U.S. is

   a. $150,000.
   b. $300,000.
   c. $1 million.
   d. $1.5 million.

ANSWER: _____
SOURCE(S): FAR 2.101

5. Which of the following is a commercial item?

   a. A nondevelopmental item, if the procuring agency determines the item was developed exclusively at private expense and sold in substantial quantities, on a competitive basis, to multiple state and local governments
   b. An item that evolved from an item that has not been sold to the general public
   c. A commercial item that has received modifications not available in the commercial marketplace
   d. A nondevelopmental item used exclusively for governmental purposes

ANSWER: _____
SOURCE(S): FAR 2.101

6. Consolidating two or more requirements for supplies or services, previously provided or performed under separate smaller contracts, into a solicitation for a single contract is defined as

   a. combining.
   b. consolidating.
   c. bundling.
   d. mixing.

ANSWER: _____
SOURCE(S): FAR 2.101

7. Which of the following are included in the definition of "contracts"?

   a. Awards and notices of awards and grants
   b. Letter contracts and cooperative agreements
   c. Letter contracts and job orders issued under basic ordering agreements
   d. Blanket purchase agreements and imprest funds

ANSWER: _____
SOURCE(S): FAR 2.101

FAR Part 3 (Improper Business Practices/Personal Conflicts of Interest)

8. The government can minimize the opportunity for buying in by using any of the following techniques:

   a. simplified acquisition procedures
   b. priced options, amortization of nonrecurring costs, and simplified acquisition procedures
   c. simplified acquisition procedures, costs, and multiyear contracting
   d. multiyear contracting, priced options, and amortization of nonrecurring costs

ANSWER: _____
SOURCE(S): FAR 3.501-2

9. Contractor's arrangements to pay contingent fees for soliciting government contracts have long been considered contrary to public policy because

    a. they discourage competition.
    b. such arrangements may lead to attempted or actual exercise of improper influence.
    c. they result in excessive overhead costs.
    d. accountability of costs is difficult to track.

ANSWER: ____
SOURCE(S): FAR 3.402

FAR Part 4 (Administrative Matters)

10. A contract with a corporation shall be signed

    a. by the chief financial officer.
    b. by the head of the contracts department.
    c. in the corporate name, followed by the word "by" and the signature and title of the person authorized to sign.
    d. by the chief executive officer.

ANSWER:_____
SOURCE(S): FAR 4.102

FAR Part 5 (Publicizing Contract Actions)

11. What is the dollar threshold for public announcement of contract awards?

    a. $500,000
    b. $4,000,000
    c. $5,000,000
    d. $10,000,000

ANSWER: ____
SOURCE(S): FAR 5.303

12. Acceptable methods for disseminating information on proposed contract actions include

    a. assisting local trade association in disseminating information to their members, announcements in magazines at no cost, and phone calls.
    b. synopsis in the governmentwide point of entry, phone calls, and paid advertisements.
    c. assisting local trade association in disseminating information to their members, announcements in magazines at no cost, and synopsis in the governmentwide point of entry.
    d. paid advertisements in newspapers published and printed in the District of Columbia when supplies and services will not be supplied/furnished in or around the District of Columbia.

ANSWER: ____
SOURCE(S): FAR 5.101(a) & (b)

FAR Part 6 (Competition Requirements)

13. The contracting officer may use competitive proposals in lieu of sealed bids if

    a. time permits the solicitation, submission, and evaluation of sealed bids.
    b. award will be made on the basis of price and other price related factors.
    c. it is necessary to conduct discussions.
    d. the resulting contract will be with a small business.

ANSWER: ____
SOURCE(S): FAR 6.401(b)

14. The contracting officer's certification can serve as approval of the justification for other than full and open competition for a proposed contract NOT exceeding

a. $25,000.
b. $650,000.
c. $1,500,000.
d. $5,500,000.

ANSWER: ____
SOURCE(S): FAR 6.304(a)(1)

15. FAR Part 6, Competition Requirements, applies to which of the following?

a. A $1 million contract for construction
b. A contract awarded using the simplified acquisition procedures of Part 13
c. A contract modification for $1 million that is within the scope and under the terms of an existing contract
d. A $1 million task order placed against a task order contract entered into pursuant to Subpart 16.5

ANSWER: ____
SOURCE(S): FAR 6.001(a),(c), (f)

FAR Part 7 (Acquisition Planning)

16. If other than full and open competition is anticipated, the acquisition plan must be coordinated with the cognizant

a. competition advocate.
b. head of the contracting activity.
c. small business office.
d. contract administrator.

ANSWER: ____
SOURCE(S): FAR 7.104(c)

17. Acquisition planning should begin

a. when a purchase request is received.
b. when a statement of work is received.
c. as soon as the agency need is identified.

d. within 30 days of receipt of the purchase request.

ANSWER: ____
SOURCE(S): FAR 7.104(a)

FAR Part 8 (Required Source of Supplies Services)

18. The Federal Supply program provides federal agencies with a simplified process for obtaining commonly used commercial supplies and services at prices associated with volume buying. It is directed and managed by the

a. Commerce Department.
b. Executive Department.
c. General Services Administration.
d. Defense Logistics Agency.

ANSWER: ____
SOURCE(S): FAR 8.402(a)

19. Which of the following is the name of GSA's electronic system that allows ordering activities to post requirements, obtain quotes, and issue orders electronically?

a. GSA*Advantage!*
b. GSA Stock
c. e-Buy
d. Customer Supply Center

ANSWER: ____
SOURCE(S): FAR 8.402(d)

20. In the event that the Federal Prison Industries (FPI) and nonprofit agencies participating in the AbilityOne Program produce identical supplies, the ordering offices shall purchase supplies from the following sources based on priority. Identify the source that has first priority:

a. AbilityOne participating nonprofit agencies
b. Federal Prison Industries, Inc.

c. Commercial sources

d. Federal Supply Schedule

ANSWER: _____

SOURCE(S): FAR 8.603

FAR Part 9 (Contractor Qualifications)

21. Normally, testing and approval is appropriate in contracts for

   a. research and development.
   b. products requiring qualifications before award.
   c. products normally sold in commercial market.
   d. products requiring an approved first article to serve as a manufacturing standard.

ANSWER: _____

SOURCE(S): FAR 9.303

22. A qualification requirement is a government requirement for

   a. testing or other quality assurance demonstration that must be completed before award.
   b. testing that must be completed before the first item is delivered under the contract.
   c. testing or other quality assurance demonstration that is always at the contractor's expense.
   d. approving a contractor's quality system.

ANSWER: _____

SOURCE(S): FAR 9.202(a)

FAR Part 10 (Market Research)

23. Agencies are required to use the results of market research to determine

   a. if detailed government specifications exist.

   b. a fair and reasonable price.
   c. the government's requirements.
   d. the extent to which commercial items or nondevelopmental items could satisfy the need.

ANSWER: _____

SOURCE(S): FAR 10.001(a)(3)

24. If market research indicates that neither commercial items nor nondevelopmental items are available to satisfy agency needs, agencies

   a. must reevaluate the need and determine whether it can be restated to permit commercial or nondevelopmental items to satisfy them.
   b. may set-aside the procurement.
   c. are authorized to pursue the acquisition as a restricted procurement.
   d. shall solicit and award any resultant contract using FAR Part 12 policies and procedures.

ANSWER: _____

SOURCE(S): FAR 10.002(c), (d)

FAR Part 11 (Describing Agency Needs)

25. Contract delivery or performance schedules may be expressed by

   a. the means determined by the requiring activity.
   b. specific number of days from the date of the contract.
   c. specific time for delivery after receipt by the buyer of each order under the contract.
   d. any means the contractor specified in its bid or proposal.

ANSWER: _____

SOURCE(S): FAR 11.403(a)

26. To the maximum extent practicable, acquisition officials should state all the following requirements with respect to an acquisition of supplies or services, with the exception of

a. functions to be performed.
b. performance required.
c. essential physical characteristics.
d. preference for commercial or nondevelopmental items.

ANSWER: ____
SOURCE(S): FAR 11.002(a)

FAR Part 12 (Acquisition of Commercial Items)

27. Contracting activities shall employ simplified acquisition procedures to the maximum extent practicable for acquisitions of commercial items not exceeding

a. $1,000,000.
b. $650,000.
c. $6,500,000.
d. $3,500,000.

ANSWER: ____
SOURCE(S): FAR 12.203

28. Unless otherwise provided in section 12.207(b), agencies shall use which of the following contract type(s) for the acquisition of commercial items?

a. any type of contract
b. fixed-price contract with prospective price redetermination
c. firm-fixed-price or fixed-price with economic price adjustment contracts
d. cost-plus-incentive-fee contracts only

ANSWER: ____
SOURCE(S): FAR 12.207

29. Cost Accounting Standards

a. apply to all acquisitions for commercial items.
b. apply only to commercial acquisitions from large business.
c. never apply to commercial acquisitions.
d. do not apply to contracts and subcontracts for commercial acquisition unless the contract provides for an economic price adjustment based on actual costs incurred.

ANSWER: ____
SOURCE(S): FAR 12.214

30. When acquiring commercial items, the contracting officer

a. is not required to establish price reasonableness.
b. can accept the commercial standard for price reasonableness.
c. must establish price reasonableness in accordance with 13.106-3, 14.408-2, or Subpart 15.4, as applicable.
d. must establish price reasonableness in accordance with commercial practices.

ANSWER: ____
SOURCE(S): FAR 12.209

FAR Part 13 (Simplified Acquisition Procedures)

31. A system whereby the CO receives authorization from a fiscal and accounting officer to obligate funds on purchase documents against a specified lump sum of funds reserved for the purpose for a specified time rather than obtaining individual obligation authority on each purchase document is

a. a blanket purchase agreement.
b. long lead funding.
c. bulk funding.
d. a charge account.

ANSWER: ____
SOURCE(S): FAR 13.101(b)(4)

32. A cash fund of a fixed amount established
by an advance of funds, without charge to
an appropriation, from an agency finance
or disbursing officer to a duly appointed
cashier for disbursement as needed from
time to time in making payment in cash
for relatively small purchases is a/an

a. nonappropriated fund.
b. general fund.
c. imprest fund.
d. administrative commitment document.

ANSWER: ____
SOURCE(S): FAR 13.001

33. Imprest funds may be used for transactions
up to

a. $25,000.
b. $10,000.
c. $1,000.
d. $500.

ANSWER: ____
SOURCE(S): FAR 13.305-3(a)

34. It is advantageous to establish blanket
purchase agreements with firms who

a. have past performance records that
   show them to be unreliable.
b. bid only on purchases over the simplified acquisition threshold.
c. have provided few purchases at or
   below the simplified acquisition
   threshold.
d. offer quality supplies or services at
   consistently lower prices than their
   competitors.

ANSWER: ____
SOURCE(S): FAR 13.303-2(b)(2)

35. Which of the following is true concerning
the use of simplified acquisition procedures?

a. Purchases above the micro-purchase
   level are generally set-aside for small
   business.
b. They can be used in the acquisition of
   commercial items without any limits.
c. They cannot be employed when the
   governmentwide commercial purchase
   card is used.
d. There is no requirement for competition.

ANSWER: ____
SOURCE(S): FAR 13.003(b)(1)

36. Which of the following is true concerning
blanket purchase agreements (BPAs)?

a. A purchase requisition is required to
   establish one.
b. Use of a BPA exempts an agency from
   the responsibility for keeping obligations and expenditures within available
   funds.
c. They may be established with more
   than one supplier.
d. They may be established even if there
   is an existing requirements contract for
   the same supply or service.

ANSWER: ____
SOURCE(S): FAR 13.303-2(c)(1)

37. When fast payment procedures are utilized, who is responsible for determining
the amount of debts resulting from failure
of contractors to properly replace, repair,
or correct supplies lost, damaged, or not
conforming to purchase requirements?

a. program manager
b. contracting officer
c. head of the contracting authority
d. accounting and finance officer

ANSWER: ____
SOURCE(S): FAR 13.401(b)

38. FAR 13.302-4, "Termination or cancellation of purchase orders." If the contractor accepts the cancellation and does not claim that costs were incurred as a result of beginning performance under the purchase order, then

    a. no further action is required and the purchase order shall be considered canceled.
    b. the contractor receives a cancellation fee equal to 10% of the original purchase order price.
    c. the contracting officer shall process the termination action.
    d. the contractor is entitled to receive the automatic award of any purchase order for the same item or service generated within 90 days of the cancellation.

ANSWER: _____
SOURCE(S): FAR 13.302-4(b)(1)

39. Unpriced purchase orders may be used to acquire

    a. repairs to equipment requiring disassembly to determine the nature and extent of repairs.
    b. commercial or nondevelopmental items.
    c. urgently needed supplies available through multiple sources.
    d. routine items for stock.

ANSWER: _____
SOURCE(S): FAR 13.302-2(b)(2)

40. Which of the following is true about micro-purchases?

    a. They may not be awarded without soliciting competitive quotations.
    b. Only a contracting officer may award them.
    c. The governmentwide commercial purchase card is the preferred means to purchase and pay for them.

    d. The requirements in FAR Part 8 do not apply to them.

ANSWER: _____
SOURCE(S): FAR 13.201(b), (c), (e), 13.202(a)(2),

41. Which of the following is true about quotations?

    a. A quotation is not an offer.
    b. Solicitation of oral quotations under the Simplified Acquisition Threshold is discouraged.
    c. Restriction of solicitation to suppliers of well-known and widely distributed makes or brands is preferred.
    d. Standing price quotations may not be used.

ANSWER: _____
SOURCE(S): FAR 13.004; 13.106-1(c); 13.104(a)(2); 13.103

FAR Part 14 (Sealed Bidding)

42. Which of the following is true concerning descriptive literature?

    a. Contracting officers have complete discretion in requiring descriptive literature.
    b. The contracting officer may waive the requirement for descriptive literature.
    c. Descriptive literature is the same as a bid sample.
    d. Unsolicited descriptive literature shall always be disregarded.

ANSWER: _____
SOURCE(S): FAR 14.202-4, -5(a), (d), (e)

43. A pre-bid conference is never to be used for

    a. answering industry's questions.
    b. amending an ambiguous IFB.
    c. explaining requirements.
    d. conducting market research.

ANSWER: _____
SOURCE(S): FAR 14.207

44. The first step of two-step bidding involves

a. price analysis only.
b. technical analysis only.
c. price and technical analysis.
d. historical analysis.

ANSWER: _____
SOURCE(S): FAR 14.501(a)

45. What is acceptable evidence to establish the time of receipt at the government installation?

a. a U.S. Post Office proof of mailing receipt
b. other documentary evidence maintained by the contractor
c. oral testimony or statements by the bidder's personnel
d. time/date stamp of that installation on the bid wrapper

ANSWER: _____
SOURCE(S): FAR 14.304(c)

46. Which is not a reason to reject a bid?

a. The bid does not conform to the delivery schedule.
b. The price is unreasonable.
c. The schedule contains an apparent clerical mistake.
d. The bid states a price as being subject to "price in effect at time of delivery".

ANSWER: _____
SOURCE(S): FAR 14.404-2, 14.407-2

47. Which of the following is true concerning electronic bids?

a. Contracting officers may authorize use of electronic commerce for submission of bids, but must specify the electronic commerce method(s) that bidders may use.

b. Contracting officers may not authorize use of electronic commerce for submission of bids.
c. Contracting officers may authorize use of electronic commerce for submission of bids only when urgency prohibits the time needed to obtain conventional bids.
d. If electronic bids are authorized bidders may use any method of electronic commerce to submit their bid. A firm-fixed-price or fixed-price with economic price adjustment contract will be used.

ANSWER: _____
SOURCE(S): FAR 14.202-8

48. Which of the following contract types may be used with sealed bidding procedures?

a. cost-plus-fixed fee
b. firm-fixed-price and sometimes fixed-price with economic price adjustment
c. any within the family of fixed-price contract types
d. firm-fixed-price only

ANSWER: _____
SOURCE(S): FAR 14.104

FAR Part 15 (Contracting by Negotiation)

49. Exchanges of information among all interested parties are encouraged

a. from the earliest identification of a requirement through receipt of proposals.
b. from release of the RFP through receipt of proposals.
c. from release of the synopsis through receipt of proposals.
d. throughout the acquisition process.

ANSWER: _____
SOURCE(S): FAR 15.201(a)

50. The process of examining and evaluating a proposed price without evaluating its separate cost elements and proposed profit is called

a. technical analysis.
b. price analysis.
c. field pricing support analysis.
d. informal analysis.

ANSWER: _____
SOURCE(S): FAR 15.404-1(b)

51. Which statement concerning requests for information (RFIs) is true?

a. Responses to RFIs are not offers and may not be accepted by the government to form a binding contract.
b. Responses to RFIs may be accepted by the government to form a binding contract.
c. RFIs are used when the government desires market information and intends to award a contract immediately.
d. Use of RFIs is limited to purchases not exceeding the simplified acquisition threshold.

ANSWER: _____
SOURCE(S): FAR 15.201(e)

52. Which statement about proposal revisions is true?

a. A contracting officer may consider a revision to a proposal that has been eliminated or otherwise removed from the competitive range.
b. Final proposal revisions may be oral.
c. The contracting officer may request or allow proposal revisions to clarify and document understandings reached during negotiations.
d. Cut-off dates for submission of final proposal revisions are negotiated with each offeror.

ANSWER: _____
SOURCE(S): FAR 15.307(a), (b)

53. The contractor is required to submit certified cost and pricing data for subcontracts that

a. are the lower of either $12,500,000 or valued at more than both the pertinent cost or pricing threshold and more than 10% of the prime contractor's price.
b. are awarded to first time subcontractors.
c. are valued above $10,000,000 and entered into with small businesses.
d. are valued above $10,000,000 and entered into with large businesses.

ANSWER: _____
SOURCE(S): FAR 15.404-3(c)(1)

54. Communication with an offeror for the sole purpose of eliminating minor irregularities, informalities, or apparent clerical mistakes in the proposal is called

a. verification.
b. clarification.
c. discussion.
d. remuneration.

ANSWER: _____
SOURCE(S): FAR 15.306(a)(1), (2)

55. A proposal may be withdrawn

a. by written notice at any time before award.
b. by oral notice at any time before award.
c. at any time.
d. at any time with the consent of the contracting officer.

ANSWER: _____
SOURCE(S): FAR 15.208(e)

56. The extent of participation of small disadvantaged business concerns in performance of the contract shall be evaluated in unrestricted acquisitions expected to exceed

a. $500,000 ($1 million for construction).
b. $650,000 ($1.5 million for construction).
c. the Simplified Acquisition Threshold.
d. $700,000.

ANSWER: _____
SOURCE(S): FAR 15.304(c)(4)

57. A certificate of current cost or pricing data

a. does not constitute a representation as to the accuracy of the contractor's judgment on the estimate of future costs or projections.
b. is required upon exercise of an option at the price established at contract award, regardless of dollar value.
c. is required for proposals in support of interim billing price adjustments valued in excess of $500,000.
d. is no longer required.

ANSWER: _____
SOURCE(S): FAR 15.403-2(a), 15.406-2(b)

58. If defective pricing is discovered after award

a. the government has no recourse.
b. the contractor determines the amount of increase and bills the government.
c. the government is entitled to a price adjustment if the amount is significant.
d. a 15% penalty applies to any overpayment attributable to the contractor's error.

ANSWER: _____
SOURCE(S): FAR 15.407-1(b)(1)

59. Pre-award debriefings shall NOT disclose

a. the number of offerors.
b. a synopsis of the agency's evaluation of the offeror's proposal.
c. a summary of the rationale for eliminating the offeror from the competition.
d. responses to relevant questions about source selection procedures.

ANSWER: _____
SOURCE(S): FAR 15.505(e),(f)

60. The least preferred method of submitting ideas/concepts to the government is

a. in response to broad agency announcements.
b. through participation in small business innovation research programs.
c. in response to program research and development announcements.
d. unsolicited proposals.

ANSWER: _____
SOURCE(S): FAR 15.602, 15.604(a)(3)

FAR Part 16 (Types of Contracts)

61. Which of the following is a true contract type allowed by the *FAR*?

a. cost-plus-allowable-fee contract
b. cost-plus-fixed-fee contract
c. cost-plus-a-percentage-of-cost contract
d. cost-plus-firm-fee contract

ANSWER: _____
SOURCE(S): FAR 16.102, 16.306

62. When is an indefinite-delivery contract appropriate?

   a. when it is not possible to estimate accurately the extent or duration of the work
   b. when the specifications/work statement is clearly defined
   c. when uncertainties involved in contractor performance do not permit costs to be estimated
   d. when the exact times and/or quantities of future deliveries are not known at time of award

ANSWER: _____
SOURCE(S): FAR 16.501-2(a)

FAR Part 17 (Special Contract Methods)

63. The contracting officer may exercise options only after determining that

   a. funds are available.
   b. funds are available and the requirements covered by the option fulfills an existing government need.
   c. market prices for supplies or services are likely to change substantially.
   d. the requirements covered by the option fulfills an existing government need.

ANSWER: _____
SOURCE(S): FAR 17.202(c)(2), 17.207(c)

64. Options for increased quantities of supplies/services may NOT be expressed in terms of

   a. percentage of specific line items.
   b. increase in specific line items.
   c. additional numbered line items.
   d. a range of quantities for various line items.

ANSWER: _____
SOURCE(S): FAR 17.204(f)

FAR Part 18 (Emergency Acquisitions)

65. Which acquisition flexibility requires an emergency declaration or designation of contingency operation?

   a. limiting sources and/or full and open competition when the requirement is urgent
   b. use of the Defense Priorities and Allocations System (DPAS)
   c. $10,000 micro purchase for defense against or recovery from nuclear, biological, chemical, or radiological attack
   d. use of the authority of Public Law 85-804 (concerning extraordinary contractual actions) to authorize advance payments to facilitate national defense)

ANSWER: _____
SOURCE(S): FAR 18.1&2

FAR Part 19 (Small Business Programs)

66. A protest concerning small business representation

   a. will not be considered for the instant award.
   b. may be considered timely whether filed before or after award if filed by an interested party.
   c. is timely if filed by the next lowest bidder after award.
   d. may be considered timely if made orally if it is confirmed in writing within a five-day period.

ANSWER: _____
SOURCE(S): FAR 19.302

67. The CO shall set aside a portion of an acquisition, except for construction, for exclusive small business participation when

a. there is a reasonable expectation that only two businesses, one small and one large, will respond with an offer.
b. the requirement is not severable into two or more economic production runs or reasonable lots.
c. the acquisition is subject to simplified acquisition procedures.
d. the requirement is severable into two or more economic production runs.

ANSWER: _____
SOURCE(S): FAR 19.502-3(a)

FAR Part 22 (Application of Labor Laws to Government Acquisitions)

68. The Contract Work Hours and Safety Standards Act requires

a. each contractor and subcontractor shall furnish a weekly statement of compliance with respect to the wages paid each employee during the preceding week.
b. that it is unlawful to induce any person employed in the construction or repair of public buildings or public works, financed in whole or in part by the United States, to give up any part of the compensation to which that person is entitled under a contract of employment.
c. that no laborer or mechanic employed directly upon the site of the work shall receive less than the prevailing wage rates as determined by the Secretary of Labor.
d. that contractors and subcontractors on covered contracts shall pay laborers and mechanics employed in the performance of the contracts one and one-half times their basic rate of pay for all hours worked over 40 in a workweek.

ANSWER: _____
SOURCE(S): FAR 22.403-3

69. Which of the following is not true concerning project wage determinations?

a. They are issued at the specific request of a contracting agency.
b. They are effective for 90 calendar days from the date of determination.
c. They are used only when no general wage determination applies.
d. They apply only to the contracts for which they were issued.

ANSWER: _____
SOURCE(S): FAR 22.404-1(b)

70. This act provides that contracts in excess of $2,000 to which the United States is a party for construction, alteration, or repair of public buildings within the U.S. shall contain a clause that no laborer shall receive less than the prevailing wage rates as determined by the Secretary of Labor.

a. Davis-Bacon Act
b. Walsh-Healey Public Contracts Act
c. Contract Work Hours and Safety Standards Act
d. Minimum Wage Act

ANSWER: _____
SOURCE(S): FAR 22.403-1

71. The Walsh-Healey Public Contracts Act

a. addresses use of high technology ball bearings.
b. applies to construction contracts over $2,500.
c. requires that all manufacturing be accomplished outside the United States.
d. applies to applicable contracts exceeding $15,000.

ANSWER: _____
SOURCE(S): FAR 22.603

FAR Part 23 (Environment, Energy and Water Efficiency, Renewable Energy Technologies, Occupational Safety, and Drug-Free Workplace)

72. FAR Part 23 prescribes acquisition policies and procedures supporting the government's program for

    a. ensuring a smoke-free workplace.
    b. protecting and improving the quality of work and home life.
    c. recycling commercial newspapers.
    d. energy conservation, identification of hazardous materials, and the use of recovered materials.

ANSWER: _____
SOURCE(S): FAR 23.000

FAR Part 24 (Protection of Privacy and Freedom of Information)

73. The Freedom of Information Act provides that information is to be made available to the public

    a. by publication in the *Washington Post*.
    b. within 72 hours of the initial request.
    c. seven years after the contract is closed.
    d. upon request, providing a copy of a reasonably described record.

ANSWER: _____
SOURCE(S): FAR 24.201

FAR Part 25 (Foreign Acquisition)

74. For manufactured noncommercial end products, the test to determine the country of origin under the Buy American Act is

    a. a two-part test to define a foreign end product that is manufactured in a foreign country and the foreign cost of the components exceeds 50%.
    b. a two-part test to define a domestic end product.
    c. a two-part test to determine both a foreign and domestic end product.
    d. a two-part test to define a domestic end product that is manufactured in the United States and the domestic cost of the components exceeds 50%.

ANSWER: _____
SOURCE(S): FAR 25.101

75. Which of the following statements is NOT true?

    a. The government encourages the maximum practical commercial use of inventions made under government contracts.
    b. The government recognizes rights in data developed at private expense, and limits its demands for delivery of that data.
    c. The government requires that contractors obtain permission from copyright owners before including copyrighted works owned by others in data to be delivered to the government.
    d. Generally, the government will refuse to award a contract on the grounds that the prospective contractor may infringe a patent.

ANSWER: _____
SOURCE(S): FAR 27.102

FAR Part 28 (Bonds and Insurance)

76. Performance and payment bonds are required or may be required for

    a. construction contracts and services and supply contracts exceeding $2,000.
    b. construction contracts exceeding $150,000.
    c. any contract for services.
    d. construction contracts exceeding $150,000 and services and supply contracts exceeding the simplified acquisition threshold when necessary to protect the government's interest

ANSWER: _____
SOURCE(S): FAR 28.102-1(a), 28.103-1(a)
& 28.103-2(a)

FAR Part 29 (Taxes)

77. Generally, purchases and leases made by the federal government are

    a. subject to state and local taxation.
    b. immune from state and local taxation.
    c. eligible for state and local tax rebates.
    d. subject to taxation only in states with value added tax.

ANSWER: _____
SOURCE(S): FAR 29.302

FAR Part 30 (Cost Accounting Standards)

78. Cost Accounting Standards Board rules and regulations apply to

    a. negotiated contracts and subcontracts.
    b. sealed bid contracts.
    c. contracts with small business concerns.
    d. bridge contracts.

ANSWER: _____
SOURCE(S): FAR 30.000

79. The head of the agency may waive the applicability of CAS for a particular contract or subcontract when one of these conditions exists:

    a. The contract or subcontract is less than $50 million, primarily engaged in the sale of commercial items and has no contracts/subcontracts subject to CAS.
    b. The contract or subcontract is less than $15 million, primarily engaged in the sale of commercial items and has no contracts/subcontracts subject to CAS.
    c. The contract or subcontract is less than $7.5 million, primarily engaged in the sale of commercial items.

    d. The contract or subcontract is less than $5 millioin, primarily engaged in the sale of commercial items and has no contracts/subcontracts subject to CAS.

ANSWER: _____
SOURCE(S): FAR 30.201-5

FAR Part 31 (Contract Cost Principles and Procedures)

80. Which of the following statements about advance agreements is NOT true?

    a. Advance agreements may only be negotiated with a particular contractor for a single contract.
    b. Advance agreements may be negotiated either before or during a contract.
    c. The agreements must be in writing.
    d. The agreements must be incorporated into applicable current and future contracts.

ANSWER: _____
SOURCE(S): FAR 31.109

FAR Part 32 (Contract Financing)

81. Performance-based payments shall be used only

    a. when the contracting officer and the offeror are able to agree on the performance-based payment terms.
    b. when the contract is a fixed-price–type contract.
    c. when the contract does not provide for other methods of contract financing.
    d. when all of the above conditions are met.

ANSWER: _____
SOURCE(S): FAR 32.1003

82. Which of the following statements concerning customary progress payments is true?

a. Customary progress payment rate is 90% (95% for small business concerns).
b. An unusual progress payment is defined as any rate that is 10% above or below the customary progress payment rate.
c. Customary progress payment rate is 80% (85% for small business concerns).
d. When advance payments and progress payments are authorized under the same contract, a progress payment rate higher than the customary rate can be authorized.

ANSWER: _____
SOURCE(S): FAR 32.501-1(a-d)

FAR Part 33 (Protests, Disputes, and Appeals)

83. Does a $75,000 claim resulting from a reduction of $350,000 and an increase of $275,000 require certification?

a. No, because the claimed amount is less than $100,000.
b. Yes, because the aggregate value of the claim exceeds $100,000.
c. No, because the claimed amount is less than $500,000.
d. Yes, because the aggregate value of the claim exceeds $500,000.

ANSWER: _____
SOURCE(S): 33.207(d)

84. Protests may be filed with

a. either the agency or the Government Accountability Office.
b. the agency, the GAO, or the General Services Board of Contract Appeals (ADP acquisitions).

c. either the contracting officer or the U.S. Court of Federal Claims.
d. Small Claims Court for awards under the Simplified Acquisition Threshold.

ANSWER: _____
SOURCE(S): FAR 33.102

85. Who can authorize continued performance in the face of a protest after award?

a. the chief of the contracting office
b. the contracting officer, provided his findings are documented in the file
c. the head of the contracting activity
d. the commanding officer

ANSWER: _____
SOURCE(S): FAR 33.104(c)(2)

86. The contracting officers shall consider all protests and seek legal advice

a. only if protests are received after award and filed directly with the agency.
b. only if the protest is received prior to award and filed directly with the Government Accountability Office.
c. whether protests are submitted before or after award.
d. whether protests are submitted before or after award and whether filed directly with the Government Accountability Office or the agency.

ANSWER: _____
SOURCE(S): FAR 33.102

87. A protest based upon improprieties in a solicitation must be filed before bid opening or the closing date for receipt of proposals. In all other cases, protests must be filed

a. within 10 calendar days of the time the protester knew or should have known of the basis of the protest, whichever is earlier.

b. within 100 calendar days of the time the protester knew or should have known of the basis of the protest, whichever is earlier.
c. Within five days after a debriefing date to the other offerors.
d. Within 15 days before the acceptance of offers.

ANSWER: ____
SOURCE(S): FAR 33.103

FAR Part 34 (Major Systems Acquisition)

88. The acquisition strategy tailored to a particular major system acquisition shall be developed by the

a. contracting officer.
b. program manager.
c. head of a contracting activity.
d. acquisition manager.

ANSWER: ____
SOURCE(S): FAR 34.004

FAR Part 35 (Research & Development)

89. The responsibility for selecting the appropriate type of contract for an R&D requirement belongs to the

a. program manager.
b. contracting officer.
c. acquisition manager.
d. R&D chief.

ANSWER: ____
SOURCE: FAR 35.006(b)

FAR Part 36 (Construction and Architect-Engineer Contracts)

90. The methodologies contracting officers shall use in acquiring construction contracts and architect-engineer services, respectively, are

a. negotiation and sealed bids.
b. sealed bids and negotiation.
c. negotiation and negotiation.
d. sealed bids and barter.

ANSWER: ____
SOURCE(S): FAR 36.103

FAR Part 37 (Service Contracting)

91. A personal services contract is characterized by

a. the annual cost for individual contractor employees.
b. sporadic government control of the contractor's employees.
c. the government giving an order for a specific article or service with the right to reject the finished product or result.
d. the employer–employee relationship that it creates between the government and the contractor's personnel.

ANSWER: ____
SOURCE(S): FAR 37.104

FAR Part 38 (Federal Supply Schedule Contracting)

92. The Federal Supply Schedule program provides federal agencies

a. sources for meeting repetitive requirements on a scheduled basis.
b. a simplified process for obtaining commercial supplies and services at prices associated with volume buying.

c. a mandatory source for frequently used supplies and services at prices associated with volume buying.

d. a simplified process for obtaining complex services that the requiring agency does not have the expertise to buy.

ANSWER: _____
SOURCE: FAR 38.101

FAR Part 39 (Acquisition of Information Technology)

93. Contracts to acquire information technology systems in successive, interoperable increments are known as

a. multiyear.
b. successive.
c. modular.
d. alpha.

ANSWER: _____
SOURCE(S): FAR 39.002

FAR Part 42 (Contract Administration)

94 Subject to the fiscal regulations of the agencies and applicable interagency agreements, the requesting agency shall reimburse the servicing agency for rendered contract administration and audit services in accordance with the

a. Walsh-Healy Public Contracts Act.
b. current year fiscal appropriations.
c. Economy Act (31 U.S.C. 1535).
d. Federal Contract Administration Act.

ANSWER: _____
SOURCE(S): FAR 42.002(b)

95. Which of the following is NOT true with regard to production surveillance?

a. In conducting production surveillance, the CAO personnel are prohibited from using contractor production control or data management systems.

b. The purpose of production surveillance is to determine contractor progress and to identify any factors that may delay performance.

c. Production surveillance involves government review of contractor performance plans, schedules, controls, and industrial processes and the actual performance under them.

d. Surveillance should be tailored to the risk involved.

ANSWER: _____
SOURCE(S): FAR 42.1101, 42.1104(b-c)

96. Which of these is NOT a normal function of a contract administration office?

a. Review the contractor's compensation structure and insurance plans.
b. Conduct post-award orientation conferences.
c. Assist the contractor in management of its subcontractors.
d. Determine the contractor's compliance with Cost Accounting Standards.

ANSWER: _____
SOURCE(S): FAR 42.302(a)(1-70)

97. A contract auditor is responsible for

a. auditing the policies and procedures between the various agencies.
b. auditing a specific agency's procedures and reporting any discrepancies to the requesting activity.
c. submitting info and advice to the requesting activity on contractors' accounting records and financial and cost control system.

d. auditing whatever the government requests.

ANSWER: _____
SOURCE(S): FAR 42.101

FAR Part 43 (Contract Modifications)

98. Supplemental agreements are used to

a. issue change orders.
b. issue termination notices.
c. definitize letter contracts.
d. make administrative changes.

ANSWER: _____
SOURCE(S): FAR 43.103a

99. "Effective Date" means the following:

a. the date specified by the offeror in its proposal.
b. For a supplemental agreement, it is the date set by the contracting officer.
c. For a modification issued as a confirming notice of termination for the convenience of the government, it is the same as the effective date of the initial award of the contract.
d. For a solicitation amendment, change order, or administrative change, it is the issue date.

ANSWER: _____
SOURCE(S): FAR 43.101

FAR Part 44 (Subcontracting Policies and Procedures)

100. If a contractor has an approved purchasing system,

a. consent is required for subcontracts identified in the subcontracts clause of the contract.
b. purchases below the Simplified Acquisition Threshold must be reviewed by the contracting officer.

c. only items on the government qualified products list may be used.
d. F.O.B. origin may not be used.

ANSWER: _____
SOURCES(S): FAR 44.201-1(a)

FAR Part 45 (Government Property)

101. Which of the following is NOT defined as government property?

a. government-furnished property
b. contractor-acquired property
c. property owned by or leased to the government or acquired by the government under the terms of the contract
d. surplus property

ANSWER: _____
SOURCE(S): FAR 45.101

FAR Part 46 (Quality Assurance)

102. A latent defect is a defect that

a. exists at the time of acceptance and could be discovered by a reasonable inspection.
b. exists at the time of delivery.
c. exists at the time of acceptance and cannot be discovered by a reasonable inspection.
d. is discovered by the contractor's quality inspector.

ANSWER: _____
SOURCE(S): FAR 2.101, FAR 46.101

103. The inclusion of a warranty in federal government contracts is

a. forbidden by statute.
b. allowed only in fixed-price contracts.
c. allowed in all types of contracts.
d. not required.

ANSWER: _____
SOURCE(S): FAR 46.703

FAR Part 47 (Transportation)

104. A person holding himself or herself out to the general public to provide transportation for compensation is a

    a. contract carrier.
    b. universal carrier.
    c. common carrier.
    d. commercial carrier.

ANSWER: _____
SOURCE(S): FAR 47.001

FAR Part 48 (Value Engineering)

105. There are two value engineering approaches, the

    a. contractor approach and the government program.
    b. Government approach and the contractor program.
    c. incentive approach and the mandatory program.
    d. mandatory approach and the incentive program.

ANSWER: _____
SOURCE(S): FAR 48.101

FAR Part 49 (Termination of Contracts)

106. A contract should not normally be terminated for convenience but should be permitted to run to completion when the price of the undelivered balance of the contract is less than

    a. $25,000.
    b. $1,000.
    c. $5,000.
    d. $10,000.

ANSWER: _____
SOURCE(S): FAR 49.101(c)

FAR Part 50 (Extraordinary Contractual Actions)

107. Authority for entering into or modifying contracts in order to facilitate the national defense under extraordinary emergency conditions is granted by

    a. Public Law 85-804.
    b. the head of the contracting activity.
    c. the secretary of defense.
    d. a level above the contracting officer.

ANSWER: _____
SOURCE(S): FAR 50.101

FAR Part 51 (Use of Government Sources by Contractors)

108. Which of the following is an example of a contract under which contractors could be authorized to use government supply sources?

    a. Government firm-fixed-price contract
    b. Contract under the Javits-Wagner-O'Day Act
    c. A negotiated contract with a contractor that has no other government cost-reimbursement type contracts
    d. Time-and-materials contracts for repair of commercial equipment

ANSWER: _____
SOURCE(S): FAR 51.101

Practice Test Answer Key

1. C	45. D	89. B
2. B	46. C	90. B
3. D	47. A	91. D
4. C	48. B	92. B
5. A	49. A	93. C
6. C	50. B	94. C
7. C	51. A	95. A
8. D	52. C	96. C
9. B	53. A	97. C
10. C	54. B	98. C
11. B	55. A	99. D
12. C	56. B	100. A
13. C	57. A	101. D
14. B	58. C	102. C
15. A	59. A	103. D
16. A	60. D	104. C
17. C	61. B	105. C
18. C	62. D	106. C
19. C	63. B	107. A
20. B	64. D	108. B
21. D	65. C	
22. A	66. D	
23. D	67. D	
24. A	68. D	
25. B	69. B	
26. D	70. A	
27. C	71. D	
28. C	72. D	
29. D	73. D	
30. C	74. D	
31. C	75. D	
32. C	76. D	
33. D	77. B	
34. D	78. A	
35. A	79. B	
36. C	80. A	
37. B	81. D	
38. A	82. C	
39. A	83. B	
40. C	84. A	
41. A	85. C	
42. B	86. D	
43. B	87. A	
44. B	88. B	